YOU CANNOT BE

SERIOUS

and 32 Other Rules that
Sustain a (Mostly) Balanced Mom

ALSO BY ELIZABETH LYONS

Ready or Not…Here We Come!
The REAL Experts' Guide to the First Year with Twins

Ready or Not…There We Go!
The REAL Experts' Guide to the Toddler Years with Twins

Contents

Prologue

"You can't stop the waves, but you can learn how to surf."
—Jon Kabat-Zinn

I CONSIDER MYSELF TO BE A REASONABLY LOGICAL, RATIONAL person. Which is too bad, because apparently, kids are rarely logical. Or rational.

For example, our 10-year-old daughter recently stapled together my last 95 pieces of printer paper—side by side by side— because she again wanted white bedroom walls after insisting for two years that I paint them with green and pink pinstripes (which I painstakingly did—12 days ago).

"I'm quite sure you cannot be serious," I flatly stated as I continued to fold laundry.

With five kids ranging in age from ten to one, it's not exactly chaos- or scream-free around here. "You cannot be serious" is a common utterance. It's also a mindset. And a rule. Rules are critical. And I don't mean for the kids. I mean for *me*.

Before I go much further, perhaps I'd better introduce myself in greater detail. After all, one's credentials are important when it comes time to heed her advice. Or pay attention at all.

For starters, my husband David and I have five children. Said children, who are referenced often throughout this book, have both given names and nicknames. Since I go back and forth, I thought I'd provide you with a quick reference. Think of it as similar to—but thankfully not nearly as complicated as—the one required at the beginning of *War and Peace*.

LYONS FAMILY WHO'S WHO

Given Name	Also Known As
Grace (10)	One, Boo
Jack (8)	Two, Big Daddy
Henry (8)	Three, The Senator
George (5)	Four, Diego
Nina (1)	Five, The Bean

Based on an old family photograph I have in my possession wherein I'm sitting, as a mere 3-year-old, amidst a plethora of baby dolls in makeshift car seats, it's clear that I've been preparing for my current role as Mother of Many for quite some time.

Truthfully, the exact nature of how I'm defined changes minute to minute. Wife, friend, driver, lunch maker, homework enforcer, virgin organic gardener, avid reader, lunatic, shopaholic, world traveler wannabe, hopeful composter, carpenter, hostage negotiator, Heimlich maneuver practitioner, and on and on. If you're a mom as well, I trust that you get this.

One thing I can tell you with certainty is that I'm wired to be more than "just a mom." I would love to be the woman who bakes and decorates and comforts all the livelong day, but I'm afraid it's not in my genes.

I'd like to tell you a story. Once upon a time, in a land far, far away (where they actually experience four separate and distinct seasons), I received a Bachelor's Degree in Japanese from The Ohio State University. Let me tell you, I use that knowledge a lot.

I subsequently became employed by a major consulting firm, for which it was my job to write computer code—and then figure out what was wrong with it when it blew up the system. This is how I got my initial training in sleep deprivation, by the way, since most computer systems seem to abend (the technical term for "abnormally end," which I'm simultaneously proud and frightened to admit I still remember), between 2:00 and 3:30 a.m.

When the company caught on that the only code I was ever going to truly understand was a bar code on a sale item at Nordstrom, I transitioned into Human Resources and acted as the communications lead for the firm's North American diversity effort. This job was, in theory, right up my alley, but didn't take terribly long to prove a most frustrating endeavor for all the reasons you can likely imagine (and many you perhaps cannot).

That said, it did lay appropriate groundwork for my future role as Mother of Many, as I spent my days balancing the unreasonable expectations of colleagues and bosses alike, some of whom I'm quite certain were *less* rational than toddlers.

Growing up, I had big-time career aspirations. International lawyer, doctor, political scientist, National Geographic journalist; they all sounded so exciting. But I nearly failed Bio 101, ix-naying the medical field, and couldn't remember who the fourth president was, rendering politics an equally unlikely choice.

I was wondering how I might apply the lessons from my time creating dysfunctional (but diverse!) networking groups to a career driving—but not trekking—through the Himalayas when something happened, the ramifications of which I hadn't fully anticipated.

I had a baby.

Three months after giving birth to our first child, I said *au revoir* to the frustrating position at the consulting firm (and acknowledged that the Himalayas weren't in my future either). In one swift, hormone-induced fell swoop, I traded my degree for diapers, my briefcase for a breast pump, and my suits for sweatpants. I learned to meditate with toys flying over my head, accepted that the soundtrack of my life had gone from U2 to Blue's Clues, and realized that quiet vacations with my husband had gone the way of the dinosaur.

Speaking of my husband (since he helped get me into this mess), we've been married since 5:37 p.m. Eastern Standard Time on July 13, 1998. David has a few quirks I've learned to live with. He has some unacceptable hobbies (the worst of the bunch advertised by a deer named Vern whose head is mounted on the wall of our loft). He stores magazines from 1979 under the bed just in case he might maybe contemplate perhaps reading them someday. He can be trusted with a spatula but never a hammer, and he has a low-lying fascination with playing all C.I.A. or war-themed XBOX 360 games with the volume turned up to the point where exploding grenades actually vibrate our floorboards—in the wee hours of the night when the rest of us are trying to sleep.

But I've chosen to accept all of that because underneath the decomposing magazines and Bambie-like carcasses lies the human form of the most fun, understanding, logical, rational, generous, forgiving, adorable spirit I've ever met.

But lest I make it sound like it's been smooth sailing since Day 1, the fact is that we haven't always had a fairytale relationship. For all the gory details, refer to the Marriage section of *Ready or Not... There We Go!*: my guide to the toddler years with twins.

If you'd prefer the condensed version, here it is. Boy and girl met, fell in love, and got married; boy and girl had a daughter; boy and girl had twin boys; boy and girl had another son; boy pissed off girl; girl pissed off boy; boy moved to the basement; girl found a good therapist; boy and girl attended therapy separately for three months and then together for three months; boy and girl went to Vegas; boy volunteered to forego the Craps tables to play Wheel of Fortune slots with girl for three days; boy and girl remembered why they fell in love in the first place; boy and girl each made concessions, and together vowed to start anew; boy and girl adopted another daughter; boy and girl (and their five kids) lived happily ever after.

There you have it.

I've been a researcher since I could lift the thinnest volume of my parents' ecru and green Encyclopedia Britannica set. Once I became a mom I swiftly exchanged books, articles, and personal essays detailing strategies for climbing the corporate ladder to books, articles, and an occasional complaint about the plethora of new products, resources, and mindsets that make their way onto the parenting scene each and every day. I wondered how any woman is meant to remain sane while endlessly debating whether or not a pacifier will cause irreparable harm to her son's teeth (or his ability to pronounce Susie Sells Seashells by the Seashore), not to mention whether I'd irreversibly stunted the growth of our daughter's brain by not taking an Omega-3 supplement while pregnant with her.

Somewhere between the arrivals of our first and fifth children I decided that, no matter what anyone else said, I could and would have it all—as long as the "all" was self-defined and based on what I *wanted* to do, combined with what worked for me as well as the rest of my family, on any given day.

I wrote two books detailing real-world strategies for staying sane while raising twins, and some of my articles and advice found a home in the *Chicago Tribune, Parenting, American Baby, Today's Blue Suit Mom, Pregnancy, Better Homes and Gardens,* and a few websites. If you're wondering when I had time to write these things, I haven't the slightest idea. All I can say is that I love to write; it's my personal form of therapy.

Over the course of the last decade, I slowly chiseled and polished my own unique approach to managing most of the chaos of motherhood and all that comes with it—up to and including a kid who has been known to frequently and without warning drop his pants in the automotive section of Target, as well as the occasional need for me to do radio interviews from the front seat of the car with the kids muzzled in the back. Don't worry; one of the pants-dropping stories is forthcoming.

I continually find myself confused by friends' notion that I have boundless energy. Little do they know, I'm Google-ing "Chronic Fatigue Syndrome" in the window next to one in which I'm Google-ing "BPA leaching from plastic baby bottles."

Look, while not completely Simple Simon, finding and implementing balance in one's life also isn't rocket science. It just isn't. Unless you don't heed Rule 1. But I'm confident that you will.

In case you've made assumptions about any outside assistance I might have that permits me extra time to find my own balance, let me clarify that I don't have a nanny. Or a frequent babysitter. Or an on-call therapist. Or a relative living closer than 120 miles away. Or a carpool partner. Or a cleaning service (though I really do long for a cleaning service that lasts more than a few weeks—more on that later—and if one showed up today and offered to clean out of the goodness of their hearts, I wouldn't turn them down; I wouldn't).

Do I have super powers? No. Do I have it all together all the time? Absolutely not. No one does. And as I mention in Rule 29 if you meet someone who *claims* that she does, I suggest you run in the opposite direction. Fast.

Do I ever flip out? Heavens, yes. In appropriate places? *Si Señora.*

Do I consume unhealthy amounts of chocolate? Mm-hm.

But you really would be amazed by how far a custom-tailored personal parenting philosophy can take you.

On any given day, I have four kids trailing me hither and yon and one fighting to get out of the front of the cart. Usually, all five of these little people belong to me, though occasionally kids trade parents somewhere between the Clorox and the Cottonelle aisles; that's normal, right?

As a mother of three boys who would each be as likely as the others to drop his pants in Target's automotive department, a set of rules, which—when melded together—create a unique personal parenting philosophy that lends itself to sanity is critical. Of course my kids' behavior differs, but in all cases, what's required to survive it is nothing more extravagant than whatever *I* have to do not to permit the mayhem of the moment to necessitate a need for psychiatric assistance—beyond what I can get from a 9-1-1 call to my sister or closest friend.

While traveling through the Land of Chaos, it's critical to acknowledge that without adopting an approach that prevents me from losing my mind every 94 seconds, I'd be forced to ingest large quantities of pharmaceutical-grade sanity. I mean, beyond the nine supplements I take before noon already.

My rules allow me to stay above the chaos that comes with motherhood in the 21st century. As of late, that includes an 8-year-old who tells anyone who will listen (as well as anyone who won't) that the person needs therapy. He's referring to speech therapy, which he receives and, therefore, thinks everyone else should receive. But that's not what most people think he means when he harshly insists that they, too, better get themselves some therapy. A few seconds ago, you didn't either, did you.

In a nutshell, my own personal parenting philosophy keeps the kids from being able to declare Checkmate even when my king is all that's left on the board.

If you're a mom of multiples, or a mother of multiple children, you've no doubt been asked two questions more times than the sun has risen: "Are they all yours?" and "How do you do it?"

I've seriously considered tattooing "Yes: 32 Rules" on my forehead so I can simply point when I see the inevitable glimmer of curiosity laced with a tinge of doubt in an oncoming stranger's eyes.

Because tattooing hurts (I know from experience), and my face already bears a few unflattering lines, this book is my Plan B.

Every mom needs her own set of rules. And I wouldn't suggest for one second that my set will, in its entirety, work for you.

I consciously developed my strategy over time by combining portions of approaches I gleaned from books, magazines, radio shows, lyrics of rap songs, and guests on *The Today Show*. Out of sheer necessity, I've even extracted tidbits here and there from Dora the Explorer and Oscar the Grouch.

I determined which pieces of the myriad available recommendations worked for *me*, and built my approach one layer at a time until, one day, I fell in a heap on the couch and proclaimed, "I'm 95 percent sane 95 percent of the time. I can stop now."

Everyone has to start somewhere. If some of my rules sound promising, give them a try. If one sounds pretty good although not spectacular, tweak it to meet your own needs. If one of them seems insane, ignore it.

Hopefully it won't take long for you to become clear on your own rules, begin implementing them, and find a greater sense of peace with which you can navigate the beautiful—if not crazed—world around you.

Enough with the introduction. I give to you my rules and the experiences that prove their necessity and value. May you soon have a philosophy all your own, tailored to your unique needs and personality.

And as my youngest son's character *du jour* wishes with almost annoying frequency, "May the force be with you."

Rule 1
Self-Limiting Perspectives Are Not Allowed

...·❦·...

"Most obstacles melt away when we make
up our minds to walk boldly through them."
—Orison Swett Marden

I LIKE TO GET THE MOST BANG FOR MY BUCK. THIS IS WHY I believe it a cardinal sin to pay full price for anything. Unless it's an emergency—meaning that I'm meeting with someone older than 11, attending an event where the guest of honor is wearing a crystal encrusted white gown, or standing within 50 feet of Joshua Jackson.

So in biggest-bang-for-your-buck spirit, I'd like to begin with a rule that is relatively easy to implement. There's a minor downside to this rule, and that is, while it's easy to implement, it also takes a while to become part of your instinctive philosophy. Frankly, the same can be said for Rule 2.

Once you master these two rules, however, they will work magic on your perspective and ability to manage nearly any situation with grace, tact, and as few swear words as possible. So start now, and by the time you finish reading this book, they will hopefully comprise at least fifty percent of your new (or mildly modified) personal parenting philosophy and perspective.

The mind is powerful. When I was seven years old, I informed my parents that the brain is like a basement. It has many rooms and niches and places where things can get lost. Like facts. And figures. And sanity.

In *my* mind, there's one thing and one thing only that can, in the end, stand in the way of your ability to do anything and everything. No, it's not the clutter in your brain's family room. And it's not your 3-year-old. It's also not the grumpy checkout lady or the neighbor who insists on revving the motor of his Harley at 5:25 each morning.

Here's what it is: a self-limiting perspective. Also known as: a copout.

Quite early in my career as an author, a new mom of twins approached me after I delivered a keynote address to a twins club. She was desperate. In fact, she greeted me with an outstretched hand and a downtrodden, "Hi. My name is Desperate."

This woman badly wanted to quit working so that she could be at home full-time with her kids. She wanted to cook them breakfast, lunch, and dinner. She wanted to take them to the park each afternoon. She wanted to be there when they took their first steps, said their first words, and beat each other up for the first time.

"What exactly is standing in your way of doing that?" I asked, sure that the response would involve finances.

And it did.

"If I quit my job, we'll have to move to another house."

"Okay? Can you do that?"

"Well," she pondered, "We could. But I really love the house we live in today."

I understand this. For the first time, I've decided that our house is our home and must be looked at as such—not simply as a potential moneymaker. Therefore, I've branched out of my neutral phase and painted a few walls yellow.

"I totally understand," I empathized. "When you take time to make your house a home, *your* home, it can be hard to walk away."

"Oh, no," she continued. "It's not that I'm super attached to our house or anything. It's just that I'm sort of attached to how big it is. And if I stop working, we'll have to downsize."

"Well, that is a concession you'd have to consider," I agreed.

"And then there's my car," she continued.

"What's the issue with your car?" I asked, quite sure that it would be challenging to keep my eyebrows from bolting upward at her response.

"Well, I've got this BMW I love."

Of course you do.

"And if I stop working, I'm going to have to get…like…a mini-van or something."

God forbid.

This conversation went on for a while, in much the same way. And you know, all sarcasm aside, I really did feel badly for her. In her mind, there were two worlds doing battle: that of the child-less, dual-income couple and that of the family of four who didn't require an 8000-square-foot house (even if she lay awake at night hoping to justify the notion that they did)!

After she finished communicating her concern about not be-ing able to finance the hiring of donkeys—named, appropriately enough, Donkey and Shrek—for her twins' first birthday party, I reminded her that she had the ability *and* power to make a choice. Her belief that she couldn't be a stay-at-home mom was limit-ed only by her belief that she had to have the big house and the nice car and the bilingual nanny (and the donkeys) to go along with the role.

I hear that same perspective voiced time and time again. "I

can't go back to school; I'm already 35." "I can't go on vacation; imagine what my husband would feed the kids while I'm gone." "I can't get a part-time job; the kids would miss me terribly." "I can't paint my toenails orange; what would the PTA president think?" I can't. I can't. I can't. On and on and on.

Different scenarios, same approach: limiting oneself based on her own "can'ts," or concerns with no rational basis, or preoccupation with what others might think. In the end, if allowed, this approach will always prove not only a hindrance, but a dead end.

However once you decide that come hell or high water you *can* do anything you want, you suddenly create a self-fulfilling prophecy. As I like to say, you "can" yourself. In order to do whatever it is you want to do, you simply must untie your "nots."

The real challenge boils down to whether or not you really want to do something. Identify a career, a hobby, or a backyard project you want to do because you *really want* to do it, and then try telling yourself that you can't. As I tell my kids, and as Henry Ford once said, "Whether you believe that you can or that you cannot, you're usually right."

Although the last time I said that, Henry replied, "That's the worst poem I've ever heard."

There are lots of things I would claim I can't do. I can't run more than a quarter mile. I can't play the tuba. I can't drive a golf cart according to club rules.

But underneath the all-too-common verbiage, what I'm saying isn't that I *can't*, it's that I don't really *want* to. Because if I really *wanted* to run a marathon (and I don't), I could. It would suck, and I might die mid-way through training, but I could do it (if I didn't die mid-way through training). I simply choose not to.

That's the difference between can't and won't.

Was I always great at recognizing this distinction? No.

I wasn't entirely sure what I wanted to do with my life when

I entered a four-year collegiate institution. I would bet, by the way, that only between one and three percent of college freshman have anything remotely resembling a strong inkling of what they want to be when they grow up, but that's a story for *USA Today* to flesh out.

I figured out what I wanted to do when I turned 27. I swiftly decided that my ideal career was in speech-language pathology. Situations continued to present themselves to me that reminded me how much I believed I'd love this occupation.

On multiple occasions, I contacted universities in the area to inquire about their programs. I bought two study guides for the GRE. I did the math and knew that I'd be 33 before I started practicing. I contemplated childcare for the kids—how much it would cost, and how we might pay for it.

Interestingly, at that time, 33 sounded so old. But here I sit at the ripe old age of 36. Almost 37. And I'm not a speech-language pathologist.

For a long time, I fell back on the copout that I didn't want to be the 33-year-old newbie speech therapist. I claimed I wouldn't be able to find anyone to watch the kids while I went to class. I mourned that the university I wanted to attend—the *only* one that would do—was too far of a drive. When all else failed, I rested on the laurels of the financial burden it would place on David and me. If none other, David was usually pretty quick to sit on *those* particular laurels right beside me, and so the dream returned itself to its rightful place: the ether.

After eight years of waffling, I finally acknowledged that underneath it all, the dream was more enticing than the reality would likely be. If I truly wanted to do it, I knew I could find a way. But a big part of me didn't want it enough.

So I determined that I'd be a speech language pathologist in my next life. In this life, I'd compromise and focus on the one thing about speech-language pathology that continued to intrigue me day after day: sign language. I'd honor this spiritual pull by making time to become fluent in sign language. And I found peace in that decision.

"I *can't* go back to school now because I'm already 35 and have three kids to care for" is a statement made with a victim mentality. "I *won't* go back to school now because it isn't the best timing" is a conscious, power-full statement. It's a choice that's deliberately made, not one that's being made for you.

Change your lingo from "I can't…" to "I won't…" or "I choose not to…" It's an easy shift, but it takes time to make it a habit. That said, it significantly alters your perspective and sense of peace with and power over your decisions.

When you hear yourself saying, "I'd love to do thus-and-such, but I can't," stop yourself. Ask yourself why you *can't*. Question whether or not, deep down, you really *want* to. As I said before, find something you really, truly want to do. And then try telling yourself that you can't do it.

Rule 2
Choose Happiness

"I most often find that happiness is right where I planted it."
—Anonymous

I SAW A CARD IN A BOUTIQUE ONE DAY THAT HAD THE ABOVE saying on it. I bought the card, framed it, and put it in my office where it's always visible.

There is a syndrome in our society. It's a mentality called The Grass is Always Greener. Unfortunately, this syndrome doesn't discriminate. It spans income brackets and success levels. Those who have little believe, "When I have my own house, I'll be happy." Those who have lots believe, "When I buy house number seven, I'll be happy." The truth is, none of those people will likely ever find lasting happiness because just when he purchases his first (or seventh) home, another "need" will surface.

Dana Fradon created a *New Yorker* cartoon in the 1970s that perfectly illustrates this phenomenon. Two neighbors are standing in their own backyards, each peering over their shared fence admiring the other's lawn. The caption reads, "I couldn't disagree with you more. I think *yours* is greener."

I've been engaged in conversations with several people who

have proposed, "Things are a mess. We need to move." What they didn't seem to realize was that most of those messed up "things" would move with them. Not literally, of course. If the school system you're in isn't pleasant, you can change that by moving. But what's to say you won't move in next door to a family whose values are completely opposite yours? If you don't care for the weather in Chicago (I'm again speaking from personal experience), you can move to sunny Arizona, but from May until October you'll want to kill yourself.

Most important, what will move with you each and every time (along with 7,590 pounds of belongings) are the ongoing negative conversations with the peanut gallery in your head.

With the right perspective anyone can be happy anywhere. The key is to bloom where you're planted. Of course there are situations in which it's best to move, change jobs, change schools, or change friends. In such cases the overwhelming need is clear, and therefore, you do it with that knowledge and the peace that comes with it. But in most cases, I would argue that people's need for every little thing to be perfect or just right (not to mention their lack of clarity on what perfect or just right even looks like) prevents them from enjoying the things that actually *are* just right—or could be with a slightly tweaked perspective. It's about seeing the glass as half full. It's about finding the diamond in the rough.

In Chinese, the word for crisis is the same as the word for opportunity. I learned this one morning while listening to the fabulous Marianne Williamson on the radio. There I was, nodding like an idiot in the front seat while passersby wondered if I was headbanging to Motley Crüe or having a seizure. We've all heard people who've overcome or are battling illness say that it was the best thing that ever happened to them. You hear people speak of spotting the silver lining around the darkest cloud. One can take anything and make it positive.

As I stated in Rule 1, the mind is powerful. Choosing happiness is one of the few actions in life over which we have constant and unrelenting control. It's an ability that no one and nothing can take away. No matter what the world throws at you, no matter what hand you're dealt, nothing and no one can take away your ability to proclaim happiness. You can stop any "negative" occurrence in its tracks simply by saying, "I am happy" to its face. You don't have to justify your reasons for being happy, only proclaim that you are.

There's an oft-used saying: "When God closes a door, he opens a window." Sometimes, in fact many times, a closed door is perceived as a bad thing when in reality it's a blessing—especially if you choose to see it that way.

Start looking at things differently. Ask yourself, "What's the opportunity in this less-than-great situation? How can I make something good come from it, thereby making it a blessing?"

By taking this approach, we can easily rid ourselves of most of our negativity. For those situations in which we still find ourselves more anxious than grateful, one of my favorite strategies is asking myself, "What's the worst possible outcome here?" The answer usually dulls the anxiety in a hurry. The unknown is scary, but envisioning the worst possible scenario often gives you a sense of control. If you can imagine encountering (and then working through) the worst-case scenario, it suddenly seems do-able. But remember, the vast majority of the things we most worry about happening never will.

Last summer, we drove several hundred miles to a family reunion. It was a two-day drive. Each way. I was super excited.

I'd filled the back seat of Lulu, our minivan, with everything from coloring books to Leapsters to what are, in my experience, the when-all-else-fails surefire happiness creator: juice boxes.

We had a whopping seven minutes under our belts when we first heard those two dreaded road-tripping words: "I'm bored."

"I don't get this," commented David. "When I was their age we drove for three days in a car without air conditioning or radio, let alone television, video games, or ball point pens. I had to hang my sweating head out the window to get air, and then nearly died from breathing in the fumes from the trucks!"

"You mean they didn't even have pens when you were little?" inquired Grace, clearly disgusted by how old we are, while never altering her gaze from the episode of *Hannah Montana*.

Eavesdropping—they're doing it even when you think they aren't. Grace didn't remove the headphones from her ears for eight hours, and interestingly they allowed her to hear us date ourselves, but not repeatedly ask for a fruit punch juice box for the driver.

When I was younger, my family embarked on a three-day drive more than once. Delaware to Nebraska (and back). In a Volkswagon Rabbit. Without air conditioning (it broke halfway through the first day, forcing my father to drive with his bare feet submerged in a puddle of freezing water that had dripped from the broken air conditioning unit. It didn't seem safe then nor does it now).

I don't remember loving the three days in the car (especially the night we checked into a Knight's Inn and, for reasons I wasn't privy to at the time, checked out no more than eight minutes later). I firmly believe that had we had all the road-trip entertainment at our disposal that kids do today, I would have almost begged to embark on the trip!

And yet here we were, thirty-some years later, with our five kids relaxing in the back of the wonderfully exotic minivan I lovingly named Lulu, their heads resting comfortably on chenille travel pillows as they ordered us to switch between Nick Jr. and The Disney Channel, enjoying an array of movies from which they could choose (but never agree on), one Nintendo DS, three Leapsters, eight Leapster games, two brand new chapter books, multiple coloring books from the dollar section of Target, an iPod, and a Trader Joe's insulated bag filled with all kinds of exciting foods like grapes and peanut butter sandwiches.

And they were bored. With 19 hours and 53 minutes until we reached our destination.

I tried convincing them that surely they could find *something* to be happy about if only they tried. They disagreed.

A few months later, we took a trip to Colorado during which we stayed at a really nice hotel. At 10:00 one evening, our phone rang. It was the concierge informing us that a water main had broken, affecting our side of the building. We could not turn on the water for any reason or flush the toilets for possibly 24 hours.

With six people using a toilet we were unable to flush (Nina was still in diapers), I decided a broken water main wasn't the worst thing that could happen to the hotel that day. Long story short, after twelve hours the hotel found us another room on the unaffected side of the hotel.

It required, however, that we pack up and move. Which was no small feat. Two hours later, as we arrived at our new room, the kids dragging their stuff and moaning about the inconvenience of having to walk 18 miles before lunch, Grace said, "Hey, Mom, look! Our new room is right next to the hot chocolate maker!"

"Yeah!" Jack agreed, "And the game closet is right there too; this room rocks!"

Henry and George said the room stunk ("for real, it smells," said Henry, nicknamed The Senator at the age of two given his penchant for shooting from the hip), but I was so proud in that moment that fifty percent of our kids over the age of four had found the silver lining in what was not the most fun turn of events. Here's hoping they (and maybe one other sibling) can find it next time we decide to drive halfway across the country.

My own consistent silver lining is my kids' health. Focusing on how blessed we are to have healthy kids allows me to quickly let go of whatever else is bugging me. Because "whatever else" will soon be a thing of the past. Grace, the 10-year-old who announced last week that she'd like to be called "Boo," and rolls her eyes so often that they almost appear abnormal in their non-rolling state, will one day find another way to express displeasure. Jack and Henry, the 8-year-olds who couldn't properly aim into a toilet if you paid them will one day be responsible for cleaning their own toilets (or not) in their own homes. George, the newly turned 5-year-old who screams at me with frequency will ultimately go to college (or, at least, bed). Nina, the 27-pound 1-year-old who demands to be carried everywhere will one day stand on her own two feet for more than two minutes.

I'm sadly aware that families face challenges every day that can't be remedied with money or time. I'm blessed not to be dealing with any of them. I hope never to lose sight of that.

I see a common approach in people who continue to smile even while dealing with monumental challenges such as illness, financial ruin, or divorce. They wake up one morning and smile, because on that day, they don't have a chemo treatment. Or because, on that day, they have food to eat. Or, on that day, they aren't being yelled at (or yelling at someone) again. They don't look backward; they look forward. And they do so with an attitude of gratitude.

If you choose to be, you can be disturbed by anything. You know plenty of people who fit this description, I'm sure, because they seem to be everywhere. These are the people who are annoyed because it's two degrees too cold, or the wind is blowing from the wrong direction, or the five parking spaces closest to the store are taken.

By the same token, if you choose, you can find good in anything. You can see a chilly day as an opportunity to wear a new scarf, a steady breeze as a solution to the leaves that have piled up in your yard, or the lack of a nearby parking spot as a chance to walk off last night's dessert. We're all entitled to a bad day, but the key is to make it the exception not the rule.

Enjoy what's around you. Find the positives. Don't allow what seems negative to have control. You are far more powerful than that.

Take a big step by saying (and meaning) three words each day and in each less-than-great situation: I am happy.

Rule 3
Woman, Know Thyself

·⊰∞⊱·

"Knowing yourself is the beginning of all wisdom."
—Aristotle

A FEW WEEKS AGO, WHILE WALKING PAST THE BOOKSTORE'S parenting section, I noticed out of the corner of my eye a book staring at me.

Called *Nurture Shock: New Thinking About Children*, by Po Bronson and Ashley Merryman, the book presents the notion that in the area of childrearing, parents have mistaken good intentions for good ideas. Bronson and Merryman, both award-winning journalists, demonstrate the ways in which our society's child raising strategies are actually backfiring.

My first thought: *Shit.*

My second thought: *Po, Ashley, "nurture shock" is not the issue for parents; the issue is information shock.*

My third thought: *I must read this book in its entirety by midnight so I can begin undoing all the damage first thing tomorrow morning.*

The book is, in fact, fantastic and I highly recommend it right along with *Parenting, Inc.* by Pamela Paul, which is equally eye-opening. What fascinates me most about *Nurture Shock* is that it's far from another how-to manual. It's more of a scientific analysis of what we're doing and why it's not working. Bottom line: if you liked *Freakonomics*, you'll love *Nurture Shock*.

Nurture Shock prompts parents to really think about the art of parenting. We're too used to reading "Do this," and hearing "Say that," and running to do (or say) it before we even think about whether it makes sense to us. That's how desperate we are for the "right" approach.

But until we know who we are as individuals and combine that with what makes sense to us at any given point in time as parents, we can't be terribly effective. It's like handing someone who has no experience with animals the alpha male orangutan and a how-to manual, telling them to get the animal dressed in three hours or less. It simply isn't going to work. And, frankly, it could be a bit dangerous!

One day, I received a chain e-mail asking me to divulge 25 possibly surprising personal revelations.

I'm so not a fan of chain mail.

This one came from a good friend however, and knowing that other good friends were on the distribution list, I thought it would be fun to learn some things about them that I didn't already know. So I participated.

I also learned that whether or not you get a chain mail like this, it's a great idea to make this sort of list. I couldn't come up with 25, by the way. Only 21. I seem to have a way with random numbers.

In case you care, here is my list:

1. I abhor tobacco. Always have. But I've apparently gone a bit too far in communicating this to my kids, as each time we walk past someone smoking, Henry very obviously covers his mouth, and then states (loudly), "That smoke smells terrible. And his lungs are

turning black."

2. I love book covers. And interesting names. I will buy a book simply because it has a fabulous cover. It could be about porn and I'd buy it if it had a fabulous cover. Or a fabulous title. Or was written by someone with an interesting name. Like, Jhumpa Lahiri.

3. I love bookstores. I can't go into one without buying something.

4. I have a stack of to-read books approximately 20 feet high.

5. I have great respect for everyone who homeschools, especially with the rash of violence in schools as of late (not to mention the fact that our daughter recently came home spouting something about the unacceptable calorie content of mangos). However, I doubt I could do it. I think I'd kill myself. That said, I'm a firm believer in Never Say Never so who knows where I'll stand on this topic in 27 days.

6. I've been watching *Days of our Lives* since the age of 18. The same characters have died and come back to life no fewer than ten times. But I can't stop. You never know when one might die (or come back) again.

7. Ditto for *General Hospital*—but there doesn't seem to be as much reincarnation there.

8. I love *Frazier, Friends,* and *Everybody Loves Raymond* reruns. I watch them every night to wind down.

9. I'm secretly in love with Eckhart Tolle. He's just so enlightened.

10. I must have lunch with Ellen DeGeneres before I die. And Nate Berkus. I also must have a conversation with Dr. Mehmet Oz. And be in an aisle seat within the first five rows at one of Beyonce's concerts.

11. David and I have an agreement whereby if Faith Hill, Julie Bowen, Elizabeth Hurley, or Kim Kardashian decides to leave her spouse for David, I'll amicably and enthusiastically divorce him.

12. Same goes on the flip side for Ashton Kutcher, James Marsden, Bradley Cooper, or the guy who played Chase Edmunds in Season 3 of *24*.

13. I plan to live to be 105 years old.

14. I have a thing for rebels. I'm a relative rule follower and danger is…well…scary, so CIA operatives and guys with pierced lips who skydive as a fun opening to their day are a weak spot for me. I've been trying to get David to jump out of a plane dressed as a CIA operative for a while now. He claims it's not going to happen.

15. I would like to guest star on a sitcom before I die (which, again, will be at age 105). One episode will suffice (unless they want me back).

16. I would also like to be in a music video. Preferably I'd like to be the one singing, but most people have let me know that isn't going to happen in this lifetime. So I'll settle for being the girl who rides off into the sunset on the back of Bret Michaels' motorcycle (and yes, he must be driving).

17. My biggest pet peeves: folks who don't wave when you let them

into your lane, people who take hours to back out of their parking spaces when you are obviously waiting, people who say "Uh huh" when you wish them a pleasant day, and people who put an apostrophe before "s" when it's not appropriate to do so. You go to the park on Tuesdays, not Tuesday's. Just sayin'.

18. I love *New Yorker* cartoons. I'll never forget the day I scored a coffee table book showcasing every single *New Yorker* cartoon ever published on clearance for $1.80 at Barnes & Noble. I couldn't get out of the parking lot fast enough; I was sure the person in charge of clearance stickers had made an egregious error. My very favorite caption is *No, Thursday's out. How about never—is never good for you?*

19. I *will* raise and train a service dog, and then sadly but proudly introduce him to his new owner.

20. I want to get my nose pierced. With just a small diamond. And I don't care that everyone around me thinks I'm nuts.

21. I say "Dude" a lot. A whole lot.

Every woman would benefit from creating this kind of list at least once a year. It provides an incredible opportunity to get to know yourself better. Trust me, I'm different in my 30s as a mom of five than I was in my 20s as a single woman. And I'm much different today as a mother to a 1-year-old than I was when my now 10-year-old was a 1-year-old. By staying up-to-date on my newest likes, dislikes, and interests, I can much more effectively nurture my spirit.

Get together with your girlfriends and draw numbers out of a hat. Whichever number you read is the number of the revelation you must share. Own your revelations. Be proud of them. Knowing and honoring the real you is an imperative prerequisite to happily navigating and emerging from the parenting years with sanity intact.

If you attempt to complete this exercise but have a hard time coming up with more than two features to put on the list, consider whether or not it is because you're hesitant to write down facts about yourself that you'd have to share with someone else. I recognize that the need for acceptance and validation is rampant, and I've certainly suffered from its effects. As a recovered validation-seeker, I can honestly profess that we truly do not need acceptance from others in order to accept and honor ourselves. We were each created for a unique purpose. Trying to be, look, and act like everyone else (or anyone else) dishonors our uniqueness. As Yo-Yo Ma, world-renowned cellist said, "The worst thing you can do is say to yourself, 'I want to be just like somebody else.' You have to absorb knowledge from someone else, but ultimately you have to find your own voice."

I tell my kids, "If your friends don't respect the real you, they aren't your real friends." It seems that's a hard lesson to learn no matter how old you are, and it's certainly a lesson that took me time to learn. But once I did, it lifted the huge weight that needing others to approve of me placed on my spirit.

Once you complete your list of possibly surprising personal revelations—even if it only includes eight items at first—you might wonder what to do with it. There are a few options.

You could put it on your nightstand with the intention of doing something profound with it but where it will only gather dust. Hey, it's an option.

A more productive option is to look over your list, and put a checkmark by those items that relate to being a mom. In other words, if you've written "I am a mom of triplets," or "I've always wanted 17 kids," put a checkmark by it. The idea isn't that being a mom of triplets or having 17 kids is "bad." What's interesting to note is how many of the items on your list relate to your role as a mom. If it's more than, say, a quarter of them, I would suggest that it indicates that you need to get to know yourself better outside that role.

Next, note whether there are items on the list that are "action items." By this, I mean things you'd like to *do*. As an example, on my list I noted that I must have lunch with Ellen DeGeneres before I die, and I also have a stack of to-read books that is 20 feet high.

It is unlikely that I can make my lunch date with Ellen a reality in the next week, however I can go and choose one of my to-read books and put it on my bedside table, vowing to read at least a page each day. Determine which of your items are actionable and choose one or two to get started on.

Third, identify your "bucket list" items. If you've seen the movie *The Bucket List*, you know what I'm talking about. These are things you want to do before you kick the proverbial...wait for it...bucket.

One item on my list that fits this category is guest starring on a sitcom. It's a great bucket list item, although one which I don't have control over being able to accomplish in the foreseeable future.

Piercing my nose, however, is another story. I've wanted to do it for years. I have total and complete control over how and when I do it. I could decide to have it done today. In fact, I might. In fact, I just made a decision. On the day this manuscript is deemed ready to go to print, I will get my nose pierced. Don't believe me? Check out my scheduled appearances on my website. If I'm in your area, come see it!

If you're struggling with this list-making project, there's a great (and somehow relatively unknown) book on the market called *Rules of the Red Rubber Ball*, by Kevin Carroll. How this book has not yet become a best-seller continues to confuse me. *Newsweek* touts it as "An adult's version of Dr. Seuss's *Oh, the Places You'll Go!*—a pocket-size guide to finding your way in life."

The goal of the book is to enable the reader to identify his or her red rubber ball—that one thing that consistently interests, inspires, and motivates him. Everybody should be able to finish this sentence: My red rubber ball is [insert answer here]. This book explains how the author identified his. For the record, I deliberately used the word "should" in this instance!

Because most people need to be guided through this type of exercise, the book now has a companion book called *What's Your Red Rubber Ball? Discover Your Inspiration and Chase It For a Lifetime*, which walks you through the process of identifying your red rubber ball. I have to say, it's one of the neatest books I've seen. It's created in almost scrapbook fashion, with well-crafted activities and questions to stoke the fire that inspires you. For approximately $20, you can get both books. It's a worthwhile investment and one I wholeheartedly recommend—even for those who think they know what their red rubber ball is.

Still struggling? (It's okay; sometimes the hardest person on the planet to get to know is yourself!)

Check out *All About Me*, by Philipp Keel. Prompting you to fill in the blank with a color you like to wear or a flower you would like to grow in your garden, this book is a fantastic jumping off point not only for getting to know yourself better but also clarifying what new hobbies you might enjoy undertaking.

When I first began speaking to mothers of multiples groups, I'd ask attendees to write down the answers to a few questions. One of those questions was, "What is your favorite color?" I was astounded by how many women had trouble identifying their favorite color. At first, it seemed easy enough for them to write down an answer. But after a bit of probing, I learned that while Mary had written down "blue," she'd done so mostly out of habit. She was quick to admit that she'd actually grown tired of blue—but hadn't had time to give much thought to her new favorite color. The realization that they weren't sure about something as simple as their favorite color sent many of these women into a frenzy, feeling as much a stranger unto themselves as the person they pulled in behind at the gas station. Sometimes, while not necessarily a surprising revelation to anyone except you, simply being able to say with conviction, "My favorite color is orange, and I no longer like daisies even though they were on every table at my wedding" shows commendable personal growth and awareness.

I must now take a break from writing, as I'm feeling a pull to put on an orange shirt and plant a row of zinnias in the garden.

Rule 4
Fly Your Freak Flag High

—⚭—

"Certain flaws are necessary for the whole. It would
seem strange if old friends lacked certain quirks."
—Johann Wolfgang von Goethe

DUDE, WE ALL HAVE QUIRKS. YOURS ARE, TO ME, INSANE.
You likely feel the same way about mine. Unless you share
them. Which is how great friendships are formed.

Case in point, if you lather yourself with Purell after coming
out of any establishment, smell a chocolate cupcake five or six
times before you bite into it, or must push your clock's alarm but-
ton over and over again to confirm that it's set for a.m., not p.m.,
you and I were meant to be friends, plain and simple. We get each
other before the formal introduction has been made.

The freak flag I let fly the highest is typically that of control
freak. I'm completely okay both with being one and admitting
to being one. I'm Type A+. I've even designed my freak flag. It's
made of 1000 denier ecru polyester cordura. The edges are different shades of orange and green. No colors bleed onto one another
yet all blend seamlessly. In the center sits a smiling Buddha, and
he's perfectly centered left to right, top to bottom (with his hands

folded in front of his chest and his head tilted 37 degrees to his left—not 36 *or* 38 degrees—precisely 37).

As some genius once said, "I have my own little world, but it's okay; they know me here."

If you missed the tidbit of information divulged in the Prologue regarding the arrival of child number five, I realize this may come as a bit of a shock—what with our already having four kids, two dogs, a hamster, and a fish in the house. But in 2007, we began the process of international adoption. I've wanted to adopt for as long as I can remember, and our entire family embraced the idea so readily that I knew we were meant to do it.

Now, when one embarks on the journey of adoption, one of the first steps is to have a home study done by a licensed social worker. As part of the process of deeming you suitable to adopt, she (or he) will likely ask to see the bedroom that your new child will occupy. By the way, I found the process by which one is deemed suitable to adopt borderline absurd. No one had to deem us fit to have a child biologically, but as prospective adoptive parents, it quickly became clear that our opinions on topics as relevant as favored method of discipline, and irrelevant as preference of plain or peanut M&Ms, were going to be equally scrutinized.

"Right this way, please," I said as I led Peggy, our social worker from heaven, through our bedroom and into our bathroom.

Peggy looked a bit concerned.

"You're not going to put her in the bathroom are you?" she asked.

Good grief, no.

"The closet?"

"No, no. Right here!" I excitedly announced as I gestured toward the back wall of the bathroom.

Understandably, Peggy looked confused.

Our plan, which had yet to commence, was to finish off a portion of our garage as the baby's room. It actually is an option on our house plans, but since we bought our home as a spec, this option wasn't available to us—which was real hard to swallow given that they hadn't yet broken ground when we bought the house.

I assured Peggy that by her next visit she would be able to see some progress, and be confident that our new daughter would *not* be sleeping in the bathtub.

One morning a few days later, I called our drywall/framer guy to ask him if he remembered that, in addition to framing out the new room, he also needed to knock down the wall in our bathroom through which one would enter the baby's room (and, therefore, into which a door needed to be installed).

Do you think his answer was actually "Yes?"

If so, you would be mistaken.

He did not remember, I thought, *which means he also didn't remember to include that work in his estimate.* I didn't want to pay anyone any more than necessary, and I also didn't want anyone to come into my bathroom looking to his sledge hammer as a means to exorcise his pent up frustration with that morning's rush-hour traffic—because there was a portion of the bathroom which would have to be put back together…by me.

Therefore, I saw no reason not to begin tearing out the offending wall myself. Doesn't that sound perfectly reasonable?

David didn't think so.

I can't appropriately describe the look on his face when he came in wondering about all the hammering and saw the reality of what was causing it.

Of course, Jack entered and promptly announced that he needed Santa to bring him his own tool set—drill, hammer, and screwdrivers—so that he could get in there with me and really help.

The framer/drywall guy was slated to arrive two days later to begin his part. In the meantime, while David was at work, I continued with my part. I needed to get a four-foot by six-foot mirror off the wall (which was glued on with no fewer than 68 tubes of Super Glue) before David got home. He had no desire to help me, or watch me, or even know that I was doing what I was doing.

The real joy lay in the knowledge that I was scheduled to leave town three days later, forcing David to live in the construction for those three days. Of course, I wasn't any more thrilled about my departure than David was; it meant that I wouldn't get to wire the lights with Len the Electrician.

The day after returning home from my weekend away, Luigi the Plumber arrived around noon to re-route some copper pipes that come out of our water heater in the garage and were in the way of the door to be cut into the baby's room. Now, Luigi is quite a character. He's about four-foot-eight, 60 years old, and has these crazy blue eyes that suggest he was conceived in a room with a view of the Adriatic sea. He has a heavy Italian accent, but speaks very good English. He's also seemingly quite fond of some English expletives, specifically, "Son of a bitch."

I explained to David that I wasn't sure Luigi even realized what he was saying. Sort of like, if you went to Italy and worked in construction, and each time there was a snafu another construction guy shouted, "Holy pasta," you might start shouting, "Holy pasta" each time *you* had a snafu, simply assuming that it was as benign as saying, "Oh shoot" (and I suppose that "Holy pasta" is more benign than "Oh shoot," so bad example, but...).

Each time something went awry, which seemed to be about every seven seconds, Luigi would either mutter or shout, "Son of a beach!" Thankfully, George was asleep upstairs and the other kids were at school.

I communicated to Luigi my fascination with all things construction, and assured him that my presence in the garage had nothing to do with a need to supervise his work, but instead a desire to see how everything was going to come together. Seeming not to care one way or the other whether he was being supervised, he handed me a hammer and told me to start pulling nails out of the two-by-sixes.

First, I had to change my shoes. I made the mistake of wearing brand new Crocs during construction once before. That mistake shall not be made again.

I then started pulling nails. It became clear that Luigi is a bit of a "whistle while you work" guy. He was humming and whistling Italian songs. So I started humming Christmas songs because that's what was in my head at the time, despite the fact that it was 70 degrees out.

Luigi mentioned that my humming was interfering with his. I thought he was joking, but he suddenly turned on a godawful loud mini jackhammer. So I sang louder. But trust me, *no one* could hear me. There was nothing mini about the amount of noise that jackhammer made.

Luigi finally unplugged the jackhammer. He returned to humming and swearing, and it occurred to me that perhaps this was some sort of cultural experience, and when in doubt, I often suggest doing as the locals do. This was the justification I gave myself for deliberately (and with my American accent) saying, whenever a nail was slow to be removed, "Son of a bitch!" It was most cathartic.

It soon came time to solder the copper piping. I saw the blowtorch, and said, with great awe, "Oh, are you going to use that?"

"Yes. You wanna do it this?"

"Yes, I wanna do it that. I really do," I replied.

Luigi did a demo on one piece of pipe, and then handed me the torch and the soldering "stuff." In case you haven't yet noticed, I never know the technical term for anything. Many items which have official names are, to me, "thinga-ma-hooches," "thingys," or "stuff."

There I was, blowtorch in hand, trying to do just what he did, when he began yelling.

"Leez! No! Higher! Lower! Top!"

Now, I thought he was screaming, "Try her!" because, as I said, he has a strong accent and the blowtorch was loud.

So I countered with, "I AM trying!"

"No!" he yells. "Higher!"

"WHAT?" I screamed.

He grabbed the blowtorch from my hand and said, "Leez, you make me nervous. You have blow torch right by drywall."

Do you honestly think I don't know that, Luigi?

He took over at that point, but for 17 seconds I was soldering copper pipe for my baby's room. I may never again solder anything, but I can say I did it once.

Three months later construction was finally finished. It was time to progress to the more creative part of the process.

First, I decided to antique the bookshelf unit I built. Yes, I built a bookshelf. But look, I'm weird like that. I love building things and my idea of a great Christmas present is a table saw. If it's not your cup of tea, it's not your cup of tea.

I got about two-thirds of it antiqued and *then* worried, "Oh dear, it's a bit busy."

I called David for an assessment and he concurred. My sister has told me for years that I need to learn when to stop, but I continue failing to heed that advice. This is why I'm not a hair stylist; everyone would leave my chair bald.

I applied yet another coat of paint on top of the antiqued portion (officially coat number four), and then applied a layer of polyurethane so as to prevent myself from getting even a hint of a desire to do anything more to the unit.

Henry loves to draw, and had begun drawing neat birds in his spare time. I asked him if he'd like to paint them on the wall in the baby's room.

"Paint the wall?" he exclaimed, "Sure!"

I then had to explain that this was *controlled* painting. He wasn't as excited after that.

The other kids quickly got wind of his impending project (because he immediately went and told them all that *he* got to paint on the walls of the baby's room). They quickly (and loudly) let me know that they also needed to have input.

Grace wanted to be the room's interior designer. Typically, she has great taste, but when she kicked off our trip to JoAnn's with a selection of fluorescent pink taffeta for the bedskirt, I knew I needed to identify another area with which she could assist.

I have control issues. Did I mention that? I had a vision for this room. And still, I wanted the kids to contribute. I wanted it to be something we all worked on together for this little girl.

I didn't want to outright say, "You have to do it my way," but the fact of the matter was, they had to do it my way.

I had some neat cards from Anthropologie (what from Anthropologie *isn't* neat?) with African paintings on them. I asked the kids if they'd like to copy the animals off the cards onto the wall and then paint them. They would coordinate well, I thought, with Henry's birds.

Thankfully, they thought that was a great idea.

Except Jack.

Jack wanted to paint rainbows. I'm all about kids' creativity, but I simply didn't see rainbows in this room. I think it's okay that I said that. Some child development experts may say I've ruined him for life, but I just couldn't have rainbows in there. After much cajoling, he agreed to do a fish.

Yes, there are fish in Africa. I think.

We began by drawing the animals in chalk so that if a mistake were made, it could easily be erased. There I was, standing in the middle of a thirteen- by eleven-foot room, trying not to trip over the twelve gallons of paint, paint brushes, nail guns, compressor tanks, and paint trays as I turned in circles supervising each kid drawing his or her animal. I wasn't worried nearly as much about the quality of the animals as I was about the kids getting carried away with the chalk (which was a very real possibility; those who know my kids will confirm this).

Animals drawn, it was time to break out the paint. First, a few deep breathing exercises were in order.

Grace finished one third of her giraffe and declared she needed a break to go online and buy one of her Webkinz a dresser on Webkinz World with the tokens she'd won the night before playing a game on the same site. Apparently, dressers were scheduled to go on sale at 7:00 p.m., and she needed to check the current price on the Hippo Topiary and the Beach Hibachi to see if either of them had gone on sale. She wonders what we old folk did as young'uns without Webkinz World.

Jack painted at the speed of light because he wanted to get it done so he could show David. Great. But I needed the paint *in the lines*. So I had to keep asking him to go get me water so that while he was gone, I could quickly *get* the paint in the lines.

Henry drew a duck. I asked him if he wanted to draw baby ducks.

"Yeah. Sure," he responded. "I'd be delighted to."

Perhaps you must know Henry to see the humor in his response. He then painted three inches of his big duck and declared himself exhausted.

The next morning, with Henry and George home sick, Henry decided to finish his ducks. George wanted to paint something. He suggested a puppy.

No.

He then suggested a dinosaur.

No.

I suggested grass, and he agreed. So there I was, with a 4-year-old wielding a paintbrush and a container of green paint.

I needed Xanax. Or a stiff drink. Or both. It was all I could do to just relax and remind myself, "It's just paint. I can fix it," while having intensely disturbing visions of paint flying everywhere.

I was patient, George was (mostly) cooperative, and all in all, it went well.

It's a fine line—needing to have control, but accepting that my kids don't have the same need to outline their drawings *before* they color them in. Or wear socks that match. Or eat the outside of their Reese's Peanut Butter Cup before they eat the peanut butter center. Which is why the greatest challenge of having a freak flag is ensuring that you don't force it to fly above the heads of your children. Rest assured that they will, at some point, design such a flag all their own. Because we all do.

Full disclosure here that the universe has challenged my ability to keep my need for control to myself on many an occasion. For example, I happen to have two boys who love to wear their shirts backwards. And inside out. I thought (and hoped) it had to do with being young and inexperienced, but alas, an 8-year-old appeared before me this morning ready to go to school in an inside-out, backward (dirty) pajama shirt. He was insistent that it be worn, and in the end, I figure some classmate will make sure that he doesn't do it again more than I ever could. Or maybe not. Maybe he'll start a new trend. Who knows?

Lest I make it sound as though one can only have a single freak flag, I'll reveal another of my own: I'm a bit of a hypochondriac. If my left toe hurts I quickly become convinced (with the help of my best friend Mr. Google) that I've contracted some sort of flesh-eating bacteria. I hold firm to that belief until the next morning, when a miracle transpires and my toe is healed. For the record, the reason I don't work harder on eradicating that freak flag is that I'm completely okay with it. My friends and family? Not so much.

What is your freak flag? Or flags? Either vow to rid yourself of them or fly them high, sister. Fly them high and fly them proud.

Rule 5
You've Never Seen It All

--------·◁∞▷·--------

"The quickest way for a parent to get a child's
attention is to sit down and look comfortable."
—Lane Olinghouse

A SUREFIRE WAY TO BE PRESENTED WITH AN UNIMAGINABLE experience is to proclaim at any point in time, "Now I've seen it all." This applies both to behaviors and parenting products. I won't name any of the products that elicited such a statement from me because, well, someone thought it was a good idea and I'd hate to stomp on anyone's entrepreneurial spirit.

But, I have to ask.

Helmets for kids embarking on their first steps? Really? There, I said it. But really. Really?

Considering that new products and mindsets enter the marketplace and the media each and every day, one should never, ever assume that she's seen it all.

We're on baby number five in this house, and so I honestly thought there weren't many everyday stumbling blocks that would faze me.

I was incorrect.

Nina (the child who sleeps in what used to be the garage) is—technically, I suppose—entering toddlerhood given that she recently turned one, and is therefore suddenly a strong follower of the I-Know-Who-I-Am-And-I-Know-What-I-Want cult. One morning around 10:35, she decided that she wouldn't drink.

Anything.

At all.

On her first birthday, as we'd done on the four first birthdays prior to hers, we said bye-bye to bottles. We don't make a big production of it. We don't force our kids to throw the bottles in the trash and bid them *adieu* or anything. We simply stop serving them.

Before I'm accused of taking away my child's greatest source of security with nary a warning, let me make clear that the kid had successfully drunk from a sippy cup many, many times before that day. I mean, what kind of parents would we be to blindside her with an organic cupcake *and* a foreign drinking vessel all in the same sitting?

Nonetheless, as of that blessed day when she awoke and greeted me looking slightly pissed and holding a handmade "My Way or the Highway" sign, she wouldn't drink a thing.

"Mix it up," suggested our pediatrician. "Try straws, open cups, different watered-down juices, popsicles, whatever."

Have you ever tried to get a 1-year-old to drink from a straw? It's a rare 1-year-old who can do this, and if yours can, beware. You have an overachiever on your hands.

Open cup? Um, no. And I watered down every form of juice imaginable including freshly juiced watermelon right from our sacred Breville juicer, bought to help David's and my cells actually survive the next 17 years. No go.

After getting four previous kids through this transition, and with electronically circulating documentation with my byline on it encouraging parents not to give in and return to bottles after saying *adios* to them, I resorted to the pediatrician's popsicle suggestion.

After dinner, Nina and I enjoyed strawberry Whole Fruit popsicles cut into tiny melt-in-an-instant pieces simply so that I could ensure that she peed at least once every eight hours per the doctor's instructions.

We went two more days on popsicles before she finally let out a sigh and said, "Fine, hand over the sippy cup." Okay, she didn't say that. But it's what she was thinking; I just know it.

And for the record, I still sat down with my two best friends Ben and Jerry and one of their decadent creations each night even though I'd had four popsicles before dinner. The popsicles were eaten merely in the name of moral support. And the only reason I had *two* per sitting was, Nina was slower to finish than I was. I didn't enjoy them in the least.

Come to think of it, the mention of Ben and Jerry is a perfect segue into Rule 6.

Rule 6
Have a Designated Treat of the Moment

---◦◦◦---

"There ain't no Sanity Claus."
—Groucho Marx

G EORGE AND I MADE A DATE TO GO TO TARGET ONE DAY
after school.

You see, the previous Friday George's preschool held Mother's Day brunch at a local restaurant, followed by a group viewing of Disney's *Planet Earth*.

I totally wanted to go; I really wanted to see that movie on the big screen. And I'm crazy enough to attempt many things. But I draw the line at taking a 1-year-old to a movie that lasts longer than 7.3 minutes and doesn't star a furry red character with an unnaturally high-pitched voice.

As a consolation prize, I told George we could go to Target and purchase a new sprinkler. Easy trip. The plan: enter, find sprinkler, buy sprinkler, leave.

I didn't get a cart (further proof of my intent to buy only the sprinkler—and avoid the Swine Flu). Nevertheless, 13 minutes later I limped to the register cradling a whole bunch of can't-live-without-this-at-this-price extras in my mid-section.

I exited $101 poorer and more convinced than ever that one of Target's corporate executives had been paid a large sum of money to ensure that no woman can leave Target without spending at least $100—even if she goes in intending to get nothing more than a drink from the drinking fountain.

In a moment of extreme guilt brought on by George's mention of his very bestest friends sitting together *at that very moment* (as far as he was concerned) in the movie theater learning about all the wonders of this planet, I told George he could get a treat at the Starbucks inside Target. (I have quite a love/hate relationship with whomever made the business decision to partner Starbucks and Target).

Anyhoo, one treat turned into two: hot chocolate *and* a cinnamon twist. 'Twas 103 degrees out, but who am I to argue with a 4-year-old who is determined that a hot drink is the way to go?

As an aside, do you think that if one knows the baristas by name at every Starbucks within a 25-mile radius it indicates that she might have a problem?

I was afraid of that.

Stephanie was taking orders, and after I requested George's items, she looked at me curiously and inquired, "And an iced grande soy latte for you…right?"

Wrong.

"I'm taking a break from coffee, Stephanie," I confided. "And it's killing me."

Not so much because I needed the caffeine but because I needed a treat. Daily. It's what gets me through. And I don't think that's at all unreasonable. If you witnessed what I experienced the last time I tried to take all the kids to church, I reckon you'd agree.

When we arrived home, I could barely contain my dismay as

George emerged from the vehicle covered in chocolate.

"George," I asked, "where's the lid from the hot chocolate cup?"

"I don't know," he responded. "I licked it and then it just...I don't know...fell or something."

"Well, it looks like you licked it with your face instead of your tongue. I think you need to wipe your mouth when we get inside."

Why wait? thought George, as he lifted up his arm and proceeded to wipe (almost) every drop of hot chocolate from his mouth onto the sleeve of his (white) shirt.

Because napkins are overrated.

I'm sure that he was looking out for the environment. In fact, I hear that the elementary school lunchroom's new motto is "Save a Napkin; Use Your Sleeve." The responsibility my kids feel toward our earth warms my heart as I shove into the washing machine shirt after shirt covered with specimens that the CDC would have a field day culturing.

So, for that coffee-free week, my treat was a bag (or three) of ninety-percent-off Easter Peppermint Patties that I'd stashed in the pantry. Before you say it, yes, I realize I could have ordered decaf coffee. But I don't see the point of it.

Bright and early the following Monday, I was again a frequent Starbucks guest. And that summer promotion involving two-dollar grande drinks after 2:00 p.m. if you bring your morning receipt? Forget about it. That promotion was created with me in mind. For a short time, I was ten dollars a week poorer because of it. And most content.

Every mom must have a Treat of the Moment. Whether it's a dessert she looks forward to after a long day, or a drive-thru item that will get her through the afternoon hours, or a bad reality show that she TiVos and watches in secret while her husband enjoys Monday night football, every mom must have a daily guilty pleasure that she can count on when she can count on nothing (and no one) else.

What is your current Treat of the Moment? If you can quickly answer this question, fantastic. If not, let's remedy this.

For suggestions, please visit the Treat of the Moment section on elizabethlyons.com. Sometimes a jumpstart is helpful. Before long, you'll easily be able to identify a new treat every month.

Rule 7
Bedlam Breeds Innovation

———— ⋘∞⋙ ————

"Invention, it must be humbly admitted, does not
consist of creating out of void, but out of chaos."
—Mary Wollstonecraft Shelley

I N MOMENTS OF STRESS, I FIND IT CHALLENGING TO REMEMBER MY
kids' names.

I mean, most of the time, I remember the names themselves. But I look at one kid and utter another kid's name. Or a dog's name. I don't know why. But this does explain why, on occasion, we refer to a kid as JackJohnBillBobMike. We've got a one in five chance of one of them being correct.

George Foreman had the right idea. When all of your sons are named George, you can't go wrong.

Back to moments of stress.

When we must *all* go to the grocery store, for one reason or another, the kids are old enough (in my opinion, not theirs) to spend 40 minutes enjoying a scavenger hunt through the store in search of unmolded strawberries, bread without high fructose corn syrup, and unexpired milk. I also think it's fun for them to be required to report in on the per-unit cost of their items. They don't.

I occasionally even find humor in some of our grocery shopping moments. Like, when the 5-year-old returns trailing the 8-year-old he was told to stick with, hollering, "GIVE ME THE DING DONGS! THEY'RE MY DING DONGS!"

And then I have to explain that we're not buying Ding Dongs. Ever.

I lost my train of thought.

Okay, I'm back.

In the interest of not having to exercise my brain any further by having to remember everyone's names during these excursions, I've resorted to numbers, using birth order as my guide.

One is in charge of milk. Two is tasked with strawberries. Three and Four go for the canteloupes (because, as you'll learn in Rule 20, another time canteloupes were needed Two went, and that didn't go real well).

Five is typically referred to by her actual given name because she's only a year old and, therefore, calling her Five too often seems wrong. Plus, I think it's only fair that one earn his or her induction into the What Number is Your Name dimension.

I do think I'm on to something. Do you remember when George Costanza of *Seinfeld* fame suggested naming a child Seven? Or Soda? Just after his birth, I suggested naming our fourth child "Four."

Forty-and-a-half weeks of pregnancy, a less-than-fun five-hour labor, and a thrice failed epidural (don't worry—fourth time was the charm) didn't collectively encourage my husband to read between my burst facial capillaries and come to grips with the notion that the name I was set on was the one we were going to use.

I didn't go so far as to suggest naming the kid "Soda," but David waited until thirty minutes after this child's birth to engage in a naming discussion with me, beginning by scrolling through his online corporate directory and proposing, "No...Oh! No...No...

Oh! How 'bout Lance? Like Lance Armstrong?"

No.

"...Tristan?"

I delivered my answer with nothing more than a look that he knows (and translates) well.

And on it went until he left the room for, ironically enough, a soda, and I called the birth certificate department and told them to put (ironically enough) George David on the official document and call it a day. When my spouse returned with Cherry Coke in hand, I told him it was George David or Four. He'd learned by that point not to mess with me until at least 72 hours post-delivery, so George it was.

Anyhoo, I digress (again). Back to the grocery store.

As I checked the final item off the shopping list one day, I requested of the kids, "Get behind me like ducks." I swerved around the apples, past the peaches and between the bulk aisles, pulled up to the register, and calmly inquired, "Where's Three?"

And wasn't I surprised when Two responded, "Three's in the Ding Dong aisle."

A few days later, the kids and I ventured out for one of our thrice-weekly trips to Target. (Still can't get out for under $100—and that day I went for only Ziploc sandwich bags.)

As we were walking into the store, I spied Four (a.k.a. George) applying chapstick.

Which concerned me.

"Um, Sir? Where did that chapstick come from?" I inquired.

"The parking lot," he responded.

At the moment he began to holler (because I snatched the tube of possibly Ebola-contaminated lip balm from him), Two informed me that the chapstick had merely fallen out of Four's pocket whilst sojourning toward the entrance to Mom's Magic Kingdom.

"Seriously?" I asked.

"Seriously," replied Two. "Do you *think* there's another 5-year-old who uses Tutti Frutti Peeps lip balm in a bright yellow tube and comes to this Target?"

Good point.

Halfway through our excursion, by which point George had applied at least half the tube of chapstick in multiple layers to every square inch of his face below his nose, he paused only briefly from his makeup routine to announce, "Mom, we're missing a child."

Big Daddy concurred. "Yeah—it's Three again."

Forty-five minutes later we exited the chamber of all things good and holy with (among other things) the Ziploc sandwich bags, a copy of *People* magazine, a peace lily from the garden center for my office, and a mom extraordinarily proud of her own ingenuity.

The next time you find yourself in a moment of chaos, ask what you can create from it. A new product? A new mantra? A new theme song? A new blog post? A perfectly justified reason to feign a really bad headache and retire two hours early?

Every crazy-nuts-insane situation comes with an opportunity to choose whether or not to make something good from it or lose your mind to it. You decide!

Rule 8
Chaos Builds Character

"I have great belief that whenever there is chaos, it
creates wonderful thinking. I consider chaos a gift."
—Septima Clark

I JUST RETURNED FROM THE HAIR SALON. AGAIN. WITH ALL
five kids.

Let me back up a tish. Yesterday afternoon, at 4:30 p.m.—and
not a moment too soon—Gracey (she suddenly insists on spelling
it that way) and I headed off to the hair salon.

Let me back up another tish.

A few months ago, I caught a glimpse of myself in a full-length
mirror at Kohl's. My first thought was, "Who lets their wife out of
the house looking like that?"

So I called David.

"How could you let me leave the house this morning in this
condition?" I asked.

"Liz, you looked fine. Same as every other day."

Not reassuring.

The morning after this incident, the incident I now refer to as
the Kohl's Self Confidence Fiasco, I looked into the mirror and

felt just plain blah. Whether it was the eight new gray hairs or the love handles or the dark circles under my eyes that made me feel compelled to do something to add a spring to my step I'm not sure. But the "something" that I decided to do was get a few highlights.

So I made an appointment with my favorite hair fixer-upper, whom I affectionately refer to as The Guru.

After driving through you-know-where for the requisite iced, grande, soy, green tea latte (which had Treat of the Moment status), I sunk into the salon chair with a copy of *US Weekly* and a whole lot of courage.

"I'm ready to try to go a smidge lighter," I informed The Guru.

She knows me well, so The Guru suggested we not do anything too drastic in the wake of what I was then calling my mid mid-life crisis. "Let's just lighten it a little," she offered. "It'll make you feel brighter. Next time we can go even lighter…if you want."

Spectacular.

And so it was that last evening, at 5:07 p.m., I announced to The Guru that it was time to go even lighter. Because if a few highlights can perk one up a little, then surely major highlights can perk one up a lot. Right?

"Are you sure?" asked the bearer of blonde. "Are you having another mid mid-life crisis?"

"Well, I'm not sure I'm finished with the last one. But you cannot imagine the day I've had. I need to go out with a bang."

Warning: Ending a bad day with a bang when the bang involves a major hair-color overhaul? Not an even remotely good idea.

"Now, I usually advise people not to do something crazy with their hair when they're in the midst of a two-month-long mid mid-life crisis," The Guru cautioned.

Do you think I listened?

Two and a half hours later, I lay rather uncomfortably with my head in the shampoo bowl. After rinsing, and toning, and conditioning (and toning), and rinsing some more (and toning), The Guru advised, "You can sit up now!"

As I slowly became vertical, I caught my daughter's eye. She'd looked up briefly from her dog catalog within which she had circled everything as a mandatory purchase for her not-yet-acquired-nor-in-her-parents'-plans-to-be-acquired dog, and done a very obvious double-take.

Folks, when you sit up from the shampoo bowl, and from 30 feet away your daughter's eyes quite literally resemble those of Bugsy the big-eyed guinea pig in the movie *Bedtime Stories*, it's not a good sign.

I located the nearest mirror, cautiously leaned in from the side so as to view only one hair at a time, and watched my own eyes grow to an until then uncharted diametric measurement.

Noting my reaction, The Guru asked, "Is it too light?"

"Um, I don't know," I responded hesitantly. "Am I glowing?"

"Well, if you wake up tomorrow and haven't gotten used to it, come back in and I'll put some more toner on it."

"What will that do?" I asked, still unable to take my eyes off of the apparition looking back at me (and painfully aware that Gracey was still frozen with her mouth agape).

I slowly rose from the shampoo bowl's chair just as The Guru informed, "It'll tone it down. Oh, and just so you know, it's going to be even lighter when it's dry."

Spectacular.

We drove home in silence. I was too afraid to ask if she liked the color even a little bit. Gracey was likely too afraid to breathe.

Upon entering my home, the boys—who normally wouldn't notice if I grew three feet or a long, purple tail—stared at me with much the same expression as Gracey had, by then, perfected.

Big Daddy was the only one who wasn't shocked into muteness.

"Um, Mom?" he asked, in his most sensitive 8-year-old voice.

"Hi!"

"Hello, Jack," I moaned.

"Um, Mom?" he continued, with a slight tilt of his head and great concern in his voice, "What's goin' on with the hair?"

So the five kids and I spent the morning at the salon with The Guru and a big bottle of toner.

Yes, I took all five kids with me for The Repair. No, they didn't behave terribly well. But only one salon employee asked me not to return with them in tow. Okay, so she didn't ask me directly. But I could read between the lines of her seven layers of blue mascara.

It's not as though that was the first time chaos entered my world wearing a tiara.

I remember the morning the alarm clock failed. This is a problem when kids need to be up at 6:30 a.m. and you suddenly realize it's 7:17. You would have thought our bed had caught fire.

"Get up! Get up NOW!" hollered David, as he threw back his Go Diego Go blanket.

"UP! NOW!" he not-so-gently encouraged, attempting to rouse our exhausted offspring.

And then, in an instant, our familiar morning routine began.

"Stop *yelling* at me!" howled Henry.

"Ohmigosh, Dad, you woke me up from the *worst* nightmare in the *world*!" informed Grace.

"Dad, it's *Sunday*!" wailed Jack.

"But I don't *want* to wear clothes," shrieked George.

"I'm sorry," apologized David. "I'm not yelling. The nightmare's over. It's Monday. You can't go to school wearing only Kung Fu Panda underwear. Let's go, cereal's on the table."

"Dad, I have AIMS testing today!" hollered Grace. "You said you'd make me eggs. I won't do well without eggs. My *brain*.

won't. work!"

"I'm sorry, Boo. Your brain will have to work on Raisin Bran today."

"Ohmigosh, this is a *total* nightmare," retorted Grace. "I will *not* get into Iowa State this way!"

"We have nine years before we have to worry about that Grace," comforted David.

"I'm Grac*ey*...with an −ey," responded Grace.

"Dad, Dad, *Daaaaaaaaad*," hollered Jack, "where are my shoes?"

"I don't *know*, Margot," answered David, channeling Todd from *Christmas Vacation* and calm as a cuke.

"Wha- Who's Margot?" asked Jack.

"EAT! BRUSH! FIND SHOES! GET LUNCH! HURRY!" ordered David, still relatively calm, only louder.

"What's for dessert?" asks George.

"George, dessert comes after dinner."

"WHAT? No dessert after dinner? But you pro-o-o-o-omised!" whined George as he sank next to the overflowing trashcan.

"Okay, out the door. Into the car. Let's go, go, go!" directed David.

"I sit in the back;" "No I sit in the back;" "No I sit in the back;" "MOVE!"

"Owwww, he *bit* me!"

"Stupid underwear head."

"Dad, he called me a stupid underwear head!"

And the cacophony faded as I slid down the kitchen wall, buried my head in my knees, and willed the coffee to brew already.

Sadly, the insanity of that day did not end there.

Because that would have been too easy.

Our family has a tradition of letting the kids each choose a birthday gift for the kid celebrating his or her birthday. I believe that this was simultaneously an amazingly brilliant and incredibly stupid tradition to enact.

After the kids arrived home from school on the day that would forever be known as "The Day the Alarm Clock Failed, Ruining Grace's Every Chance of Admission into Iowa State," I took Grace, Jack, and Henry to Walmart to purchase George's birthday gifts. The mere fact that I entered Walmart, period, was laughable; however, their selection of bikes blows our local Target's out of the water so I had no choice. I quickly picked out a two-wheel bike for the birthday boy ("WITH training wheels, Mom" ordered The Senator), and we made our way down the toy aisles.

One of the brilliant aspects of this tradition is that the kids have always enjoyed buying each other gifts. I thought, therefore, that this would be a relatively easy outing.

I was wrong.

We struggled with three primary issues. First, the immediate selection by my children of toys that, for one reason or another, simply wouldn't work. I will admit that I'm most impressed by my ability to look at a toy—any toy—and immediately discern with near clairvoyance whether or not the toy will work for a 5-year-old boy. The bottom line: most won't.

"Hey Mom?" called Grace from three aisles over. "How about this game? It's called 'Fact or Crap'."

My response was entirely appropriate. "Who the hell named *that* game?"

I suppose my language slip went right over her head because she responded, "Um, probably the person who invented the game?"

From there arose issue number two: the boys' suggestions of a whole slew of toys that were just plain wrong.

A Star Wars light saber?

No.

Play-doh?

Absolutely not.

A Pirates of the Caribbean Sword?

Yeah, no.

Toys with 150 pieces or that cost $150?

No again.

I quickly figured out the mentality with which Henry was shopping. He'd suggest an item, to which I'd respond, "No, Henry, I don't think George will like that."

"Well, that's okay," responded Henry. "*I'll* like it!"

Super.

Grace, who was the only one looking without ulterior motives, simply could not find the "perfect" gift. After one hour, I said, "Grace find a present. Any present. I don't care what it costs." She quickly decided on a battery-powered baby pig that George could feed. I wasn't sure about it; I was also too delirious to really care.

In parenting, chaos is part of the territory. The fact of the matter is that you birth chaos right after the placenta. The doctor doesn't tell you because it's too scary; your hormones can't take any more at that moment. A few hours or days (or weeks) later, when your hormones *can* take it, the doctor is unavailable to enlighten you because she's at home dealing with her own chaos.

Once you accept that chaos is inevitable, it's quite liberating. Because then—and only then—you can begin floating above it.

Rule 9
Float Above Insanity

"Just keep swimming. Just keep swimming."
—Dori, in Finding Nemo

I HAVE ALWAYS FOUND GIFT CARDS TO BE A FANTASTIC IDEA. Until, that is, one has to take the young, eager recipient to the appropriate store to use it. And hope he understands that a $10 gift card can't be used to purchase a $60 item.

Or a $160 item.

As it turns out, quality is hard to find for under $10. Let me clarify. If you're under the age of 9, quality is hard to find for under $10. Me? Lots of things under $10 make me ecstatic: a venti Frappaccino, a pint of Ben & Jerry's Americone Dream, a box of BandAids that aren't covered with images of Dora and Boots; the list goes on.

Henry recently received (from us) a $10 gift card to Toys R Us. I won't say how he earned the gift card because it's absurd. Okay, fine, he earned it by agreeing twenty times to properly put away his laundry—within six hours of being asked—instead of hiding it under someone's bed, okay? Call it bribery; call it positive coercion. I'm fine with either moniker.

Anyway, one afternoon we entered The Kingdom of Hell so Henry could spend his gift card.

He had 45 minutes before I had to (again) be in The Guru's chair. My earlier transformation from brunette to blond was, in the end, too much to maintain. I mean, three hours in a salon chair every four weeks? No.

"Jack, come with me," ordered Henry. "We'll look in the Transformer aisle."

"Henry, I have a great idea," suggested Jack. "How about if you just give *me* your gift card."

Ohmigod.

And then Henry seemed like he was thinking about it!

"What will you give me as a trade?" he asked.

"No, no, no," I interjected. "It's Henry's gift card. Henry, if you're going to give it to Jack, we're not doing this again."

"You mean we get to do it again?" he asked, eyes dancing.

"Just start looking, please. The clock is ticking."

George was, and had been for nearly 80 seconds, slapping me on the thigh.

"Mom! Mom! I have $10 too—from my birthday!"

'Twas true.

"George," I responded, "stop hitting me. If you can find something acceptable for $10 or less in the next 42 minutes, we'll talk about it."

Jack and Henry were together. Grace and George were together. Nina and I had four minutes of unadulterated peace and quiet.

Until Nina became concerned because Jack was out of her sight.

"JAAAACK! JAAAACK!" she screamed. Over and over and over until Jack popped out of Aisle 17A and stated, "Nina, I'm right here!"

Which is precisely where he was ordered to stay because it was the only way to keep the 1-year-old from screaming "JAAACK!" for the next 41 minutes.

In my peripheral vision, I spied George running toward us.

"This, Mom," he stated breathlessly. "I want this whip."

No.

The next 38 minutes were filled with requests to purchase everything from a $40 SpongeBob Ukelelee to Moon Shoes to a 3-foot-high skateboard ramp. No, No, and No.

"How about this, George?" I hopefully suggested, pointing to a cartoon that was, in my youth, über popular.

"That ghost is weird."

"It's Casper for God's sake!"

I took a moment to transport myself to the set of *iCarly* as I announced, "Guys, we're finished in 5...4...3...2..."

"Fine. I'll get these darts," announced Henry. Because they were magnetized and therefore not likely to be inserted into anyone in a moment of rage, I agreed.

George let loose every ounce of sadness he'd stored up during the previous seven hours over the fact that, in 45 minutes in the biggest toy store for hundreds of miles, he could agree to not one acceptable item under $10. And I'm relatively liberal. If it doesn't shoot at someone, curse at someone, or whip someone, I'm usually okay with it.

As we walked across the parking lot, I offered, "George, your constant happiness is always so heartwarming."

"You mean my SADNESS!!!" corrected George.

My bad.

And I know you're not going to believe that the next part happened, but I swear to it. I turned on the radio to find a song with which to sing along. As luck would have it, the station was set to Oprah Radio, and Dr. Laura Berman's show was on the air.

"Jim," Dr. Laura asked, "are you satisfied with your sex life?"

I went into a manic frenzy, first turning the radio way up, then the heat on, then the windshield wipers to mach speed, all in an effort to change the channel before anyone asked, "Mom, what's a sex life?" Because, truth be told, I wouldn't know.

There are a few strategies I employ almost every time I leave the house with the kids. They are listed in order of implementation, and they work well enough that the kids haven't yet caught on.

First, I sing to myself. It works well. James Baraz, author of *Awakening Joy: 10 Steps That Will Put You on the Road to Real Happiness* believes, "It's hard to stay in a funk if you're singing regularly." As reported in an article in *Health* magazine, it was recently discovered that "an organ in the inner ear (that responds to singing sounds) is connected to a part of the brain that registers pleasure." For the record, this does not mean that those *around* you will derive pleasure from your singing, per se. So invite them to join in or something. They'll quickly discover such inner ear happiness that they won't care that you're overwhelmingly off-pitch.

Second, I talk to myself. I've learned that I'm not the only one by a long shot. Moms everywhere are talking to themselves in the stores, pretending that they're talking to the kid they have in the stroller or the grocery cart. But I know better.

Third, I smile as big as I can and then try to catch a glimpse of myself in a mirror, which usually makes me crack up. It's hard to yell or feel too angry when you're smiling. It also usually prompts the kids to stop what they're doing and ask me, using their most embarrassed tone, what *I'm* doing. If I need something to smile about, I pull out my BlackBerry (as long as I'm not driving!) and go to my bookmarked In Case of Emergency videos on YouTube. The one of the "serious baby" (which you can easily locate by doing a YouTube.com search on the same two words) is usually all it takes.

Fourth, I go to the next aisle over and pretend the kids aren't

mine. For example, when Henry (the 8-year-old who thinks everyone needs therapy) responds to the news that he cannot get a blue
Gatorade at Lowe's by getting really excited (and by really excited
I mean flailing all appendages *a la* Elaine Benes on a dance floor),
I simply turn the corner, and continue walking while acting concerned and pondering aloud, "I wonder where that poor child's
mother is?"

When things get really insane, I pull out the big guns. These
guns are reserved. I can't pull them out all the time or they won't
work when I really need them.

One trick I've had great success with is using big words. The
kids don't understand them, but this sleight-of-mouth reminds
them that I'm smarter than they are (and I intend to reinforce this
belief as long as I can). Sometimes, when I'm lucky, they are confused into complete silence. Some of my most triumphant old
standbys are:

"Don't even think about absquatulating something in here."

"I hear a borborygm; who did that?"

"Go look for a bowyang for your pants."

"Has anyone seen a bumbershoot?"

A word of warning: you might think that when things are at
their worst, it's okay to swear under your breath. But it isn't. Because as someone once said, "Children seldom misquote. In fact,
they usually repeat word for word what you shouldn't have said."
In those moments, someone will inevitably respond, "WHAT did
you just say, Mom?" and then announce, "Guys, did you hear
that? Mom just said dammit she's going to freakin' kill herself." If

possible, they'll deliver this announcement even more loudly than whatever got you swearing in the first place.

Rule 10
Remember, the Sun Always Shines on TV

"In the 80s, A-Ha had a hit song by the same name.
I doubt they realized how brilliant a title it was."
—Jen, mother of four

JUST BECAUSE A SITUATION APPEARS BETTER THAN YOURS IN ONE way, shape, or form doesn't mean that it is. As they say, be careful what you wish for (and be grateful for what you have).

One thing I often wish for (but rarely have) is time to get myself ready each morning—beyond being fully clothed. How, I ask you, does any mother of young children manage to look good—*really* good—more than once per week (or two)?

Seriously.

There I was in T.J. Maxx with my then-9-month-old (who was still in *her* pajamas), and I must admit that I was feeling relatively good about myself. For one, I was wearing jeans, not yoga pants. For another, my hair was, yes, in a ponytail, however I showered that morning so it was in a nice slicked-back bun-like thingamahooch instead of hanging like an abandoned horse's unkempt tail. I even put on chapstick that, supposedly, provides a nice little sheen (though I really don't think it does).

All was going beautifully when who did I spy?

Penelope Perfect.

Penelope Perfect is the mom who makes many moms feel, at least momentarily, inadequate. Especially moms who *used* to have time to dry their hair but now, suddenly thrust into the one-dimensional role of *mamacita*, catch themselves in the mirrors at Target and gasp. Think Bree Van de Kamp of *Desperate Housewives*.

Now you understand *exactly* who I'm talking about, don't you?

Speaking for myself, the Penelope Perfects of the world render me far more curious than sad.

Like, at what time did this woman rise to look this way? And at what time must she begin her bedtime routine to get all that crap off her face?

There she was, slow motion in her Seven Brand jeans (size: negative something), adorable (and perfectly pressed) sheer ruffle shirt, four-inch heels (she was at least five-foot-ten to begin with), the perfect makeup shades applied in all the right places, hair as bouncy and shiny as that in a Pantene commercial. (I should also point out that her daughter, under one year of age, was also picture perfect in her trendy stroller, pressed Polo dress, hair bows—even though she was nearly bald—and little baby UGGs.)

Now, back in the day, coming upon the Penelope Perfects of the world ruined said day. They made me feel lazy and frumpy and lumpy in all the wrong places.

But ladies, a new day has begun (can you hear Miss Celine Dion professing it through song right this very second?).

Maybe Penelope has a nanny. Maybe she has a hair stylist and makeup artist living on the premises. Maybe she has a tailor named Svetlana customizing her clothing to perfection. And a housecleaner named Betty who's dusting while she's touching up her pedicure.

Or maybe, just maybe, her appearance is more of a priority for her than mine clearly is to me. Maybe she is as self-conscious as an elephant in a bikini. Maybe Betty cleans her house because Penelope has horrible asthma, and the dust prevents her from safely doing it herself. Okay, that last one was a stretch. But I'm trying to give Penelope the benefit of the doubt here. As Hugh MacLeod said, "Every person has their own personal Mt. Everest to climb." Penelope's simply isn't in the natural beauty department!

Let's be honest. I *could* wake up each morning and "do" myself. I could. I could rise at 5:30 and start the process. And I'll admit that when I do (for whatever asinine reason) it feels great. But I enjoy sleep. I mean, I *really* enjoy sleep.

The truth of the matter is that I simply don't *choose* to primp myself each day. I'm very comfortable in my yoga pants with my hair in a ponytail—whether glamorous or unruly. My legs feel better at day's end having worn spit-up covered crocs than they would having been shoved into four-inch stilettos.

As I shimmied past Penelope in the bathing suit aisle (are you kidding me?), I smiled and said, "I love your shirt!" And, while you might expect—based purely on stereotypes—that she would have said, "Mm, thanks" with eyes down and nose up, she instead replied, "Oh my gosh! Thank you so much!" as though she had begun that very morning in prayer that someone would pay her a compliment before sundown. Maybe that's how her inner mom survives at this point—deriving validation from the positive opinions of others.

And with that in mind, I think she should strut her stuff all the livelong day. I was even inspired to consider blow-drying my hair the next day.

But I ain't getting out of these yoga pants anytime soon.

When I say that the sun always shines on TV, I'm again referring to the Grass is Always Greener mentality. The women in fashion magazines look great because there's airbrushing involved. The Brady Bunch appeared to be happy while enjoying a sing-along on the way to the Grand Canyon—BECAUSE IT WAS SCRIPTED! (And unless you've had you head in the sand, you know what was really going on behind those scripted scenes.)

Sometimes, the neighbor next door (or the fellow shopper in T.J. Maxx) appears to have it all together. Her makeup is perfect. Her clothes are ironed. Her hair is highlighted to perfection. It's important to remember that we don't know what goes on behind closed doors.

Every person and every family has challenges. Some people wear them on their sleeves; others sweep them under their finest rug where they plan to hide them until the end of time. But everyone has them.

When you find yourself wishing your life was more like this person's or that person's, take a moment to be grateful for what you have. Close your eyes and identify three things to voice gratefulness toward. In my case, reminding myself of my kids' health, our cozy (albeit cluttered) home, and a husband who no longer minds cleaning toilets works every time.

Rule 11
You Cannot Be Serious

<hr />

"Do not take life too seriously.
You will never get out of it alive."
—Elbert Hubbard

JULY 29 BEGAN IN MUCH THE SAME WAY EVERY OTHER morning begins—with a glorious sunrise and complaints about available breakfast fare.

"Mom," whispered Four, as though whispering could make the question more palatable (sadly, it can), "can I have chocolate chips for breafkast?"

(In case you're wondering, that's not a typo. There may be typos in this book, but that's not one of them. That's how all of our kids pronounce breakfast: "breafkast." After a while, it starts to sound totally normal. Try it and see for yourself.)

I shall now continue my story.

"Um, no," I sleepily replied, tossing a pillow over my head in hopes of softening his anticipated response.

"But," continued George, still whispering, "that's all we have!"

Alas, he was nearly correct. Chocolate chips, half a bag of Fritos, and leftover steamed peas do not provide breakfast for six.

A few hours—and six small bowls of steamed peas—later, we were off to the grocery store. I love summertime grocery shopping in Arizona. The kids do, too. My goal was two-fold. First, exit the store before the thermostat hit 114. Second, and far less critical (and less likely), stay calm amidst the chaos that ensues when I take five kids grocery shopping in summertime—or anytime, really—in Arizona.

My *kids'* goal for this trip was three-fold. First, annoy the hell out of their mother. Second, annoy the hell out of every other shopper. Third, and most critical, convince an employee to request that I shop by myself in the evenings from now on.

The front doors glided open and almost on cue it began.

"Can I get this snack bar?" "Why does he get *that* snack bar?" "How come you never let me push the cart? That crash was an asskident!"

"You cannot be serious," I muttered, further consoling myself by initiating Chaos Survival Strategy #3: singing to myself. I sang "Love Me Do" along with not only The Beatles, who were streaming from the store's sound system, but also an employee in the vitamin aisle. As I practiced my vibrato on the pleeeeeeeeeaaaaaaase before "love me do," I almost lulled myself into a tranquil trance.

"Mom, I have to poop."

I was so close.

Forty-five minutes later, my overflowing cart and I prepared to make our way to checkout when what did I spy? A gift, ladies and gentlemen. A true gift.

It was a display stand I'd never before seen. A mirage that popped up in the Desert of Despair. A standalone cardboard table that held a supply of what appeared to be juice boxes.

But they were not juice boxes at all.

For each one contained a single serving of what we refer to in our house as an adult beverage.

I stood and stared, taking in every well-placed and perfectly stacked box. Every well-crafted word of advertising. Obviously, their target isn't middle-aged men darting into the grocery at noon for a custom-made sandwich and a Coke. Clearly, their marketing team is genius.

I mean, it's juice—of the adult variety, yes, but that's really just a minor detail—in a juice-box-like carton (minus the straw, but that can easily be added; I have 250 in my pantry). Single servings of chardonnay in a box the color of your choosing. Red, orange, yellow: which one is calling you this fine morning? I mean, you can recycle the box. There's nothing they haven't thought of!

As I slowly continued on, my eyes still riveted on the display, I asskidentally bumped into a fellow, frazzled mom.

"Did you see the chardonnay juice boxes?" I asked.

"WHERE!" she demanded, orphaning both her cart and her children, who continued blocking the aisle by creating faux snow angels between the complimentary coffee and the bins of bulk fructose.

We then stood there together, she and I, taking in the brilliance of what stood before us.

"Have a glass with Alice," offers their logo. "Enjoy anywhere. Anytime."

I have one question and one question only for Alice: does the produce section of the grocery store qualify?

A few months later, David's job was, unfortunately, a casualty of the economic downturn. In the short term, this was terrific because we'd passed in the night for, like, nine years, and we thoroughly enjoyed having our days to spend together as well as the bit of extra flexibility it provided whilst managing five children (as in, thank you that I don't have to again take all five children with me to the gynecologist).

We decided we'd worry about the long-term later. David is spectacularly good at what he does (even though I'm not completely clear on *what* he does), and we trusted that something would work out. But he decided that, for a few months, he could be quite happy as one of the many men at the park who stand around and kibitz about how long they've been out of work.

I told David not to worry about even browsing the Want Ads for a few weeks. "It's been a long couple of years," I said, as though he needed reminding. "Take some time and enjoy the kids and your free time. Go hunt something." (No, I can't believe I suggested that either.)

One morning we dropped off the kids at school and went to Target. We were trying to stimulate the economy; is that so bad? I suggested we get some cans of soup for dinner. You know, to conserve cash.

"I don't want to buy cans of soup. I want to make my own soup," David announced.

Okay?

"But I don't know what to make. I can't focus. I don't have a recipe. Can we go home right now and let me look through cookbooks and come up with something, and then we can come back?"

No.

He threw some items in the cart, and agreed to figure it out later.

We then got to the toy aisle.

"Oh, look at the Lego sets," he said, more as a statement unto himself than a request of me. "These are fantastic. The boys would love these."

"David, have you noticed how many pieces that kit has? 753. Have you lost your mind?"

"I'm just saying—"

I had no idea what he was just saying. I was already two aisles over.

"David," I inquired (having rejoined him), "didn't you say you needed socks?"

"Yes, but we're not spending money on socks. Can't you darn them?"

I almost didn't acknowledge that I'd heard him, but my second personality took over before I could stop her.

"This is the 21st century. No one darns socks. Buy a freaking bag of socks."

"That's okay," he answered. "Socks can wait."

Okay?

The conversation down every subsequent aisle went something like this:

"David, we need wrapping paper."

"Can't we make that?"

No.

"David, we need infant formula."

"Can't you make that?"

No.

"David, we need shampoo."

"Can't you make that?"

No.

"Liz, I need eggnog."

Yeah, No.

By the time we exited, I said, "David, watcha doin' this afternoon?"

"Nothing, why?"

"Oh, I don't know. Feel like job hunting?"

I highly recommend reserving a serious attitude for those few occasions that truly require it. The reality is that not much in life needs to be taken seriously. Most of it will pass.

If you can laugh or find something positive in the not-so-great moments as often as possible, those occasions during which a serious response is all you can muster will not only be few and far between but far easier to manage.

Rule 12
Cleanliness is Overrated

"Cleaning your house while your kids are still growing
up is like shoveling the walk before it stops snowing."
—Phyllis Diller

IN THE INTEREST OF FULL DISCLOSURE, I'M WILLING TO RELEASE
some controversial news.

After 9.25 years of parenting, I finally broke down and hired a
cleaning service. And, truthfully, one could usually find me cleaning *with* the cleaning ladies on days when I was home because I
was so uncomfortable lounging on the couch in my UGGs eating
bon bons (because, as you're no doubt aware, that's what stay-
at-home moms do all day) while these wonderful women were
scrubbing God-knows-what off every surface of my home.

Anyhoo, the economy tanked, and simply stated, paying a
cleaning service was a hard pill to swallow whilst my neighbors were waving from their U-Hauls. Plus, in our own home it
was getting dangerously close to the point of being able to pay
the cleaning ladies or the gas station. Without gasoline, I could
not escape.

So after just over nine years of waiting for the day when I could finally stomach the idea of paying someone to clean my house, we said goodbye to the wonderful ladies with the miraculous floor cleaner.

The joy of being responsible for cleaning our own filth was abruptly reinstated.

Which I don't believe a mother with any number of children over the age of three should have to enjoy alone.

After all, they weren't *my* 17 mateless shoes strewn about, nor was it *my* dirty laundry stealthily stuffed under the sink. So one Tuesday I said, "Kids, it's time to clean." They were super excited.

Big Daddy, as I call the oldest of our twins because you can usually find him cleaning, tending to the baby, or cooking a 5-star meal for seven, ran for the mop and got started (yes, he's available for hire—but his rates are somewhat unreasonable).

Big Daddy is the exception, not the rule. When I asked our oldest simply to remove her shoes from the bookshelf, she looked at me as though I'd asked her to dismantle the bookshelf, paint it purple, and put it back together backwards and upside down.

After asking the 5-year-old to put his cups in the sink (all nine of them—from breakfast alone), every muscle below his neck mysteriously atrophied and he fell into his favorite puddle of pity on the floor by the trash can.

Then there's The Senator, who was asked to do nothing more than clean the Cheerios off his chair, but quickly came up with the completely unacceptable solution of calling the dog and pointing at his cereal-covered chair encouraging Humphrey to "Eat, boy, eat."

The main reason I love cleaning services is that once they've finished, your entire house is—if even only for a few minutes—clean. Every room. Every countertop. Every toilet. If you could see my kitchen island right now, you might pull a Monica Geller and show up with cleaning products in hand. It's that bad. And I'd take the time to clean it, except that I already know from past acts of futility that it would be back to its usual state before I could even exclaim, "Wow! I never knew the island countertop had such cool flecks of mica in it!"

If my happiness were dependent upon the house being clean even half the time, I'd have to sell something illegal in order to pay the cleaning service. Because with five kids in the house (three of them boys), it won't get (and stay) clean unless I clean 24/7. Literally. And don't think I haven't considered it.

So I've come to accept that the house will be a pit to some degree for the next few years. I manage that acceptance in the following ways.

First, I resort to Rule 26: pick battles wisely. In our house, the kids' rooms are all upstairs. David's and mine is downstairs. This makes it somewhat easy on occasion to simply pretend the upstairs doesn't exist.

When I *do* venture up there, I traditionally begin involuntarily hyperventilating, but as long as their rooms aren't at risk of being condemned by the health department, I don't worry about them too much. Their bathrooms are another story because, well, it's just gross to have toothpaste everywhere and toilets in such a state that they're probably more disgusting than those in a maximum security prison.

We reserve one bathroom in the house for "adults only" so that when guests come over, they have a facility they can use without fear of contracting a staph infection. We keep the door to this particular bathroom locked, but aren't terribly surprised when George insists that he *did* wash his hands—"in that bathroom you keep locking. But that's okay; I just use a paperclip to unlock it!"

I wish I could say we were proud.

We also assign the kids weekend chores. We then prepare for the onslaught of complaints about why it's not fair that they have to clean the messes they've made. After all, "Our friends don't have to clean."

Of course they don't. They live with Penelope Perfect. And they have Betty.

Even though I don't yet have one, I hear that the Roomba and iRobot are great additions to any mom's cleaning closet, and I do plan to get one of them simply so that I can lie on the couch in my UGGs with my bon bons while a robot vacuums up sand, sprinkles, and spit.

Rule 13
Go With Your Gut

"Believe nothing, no matter where you read it or who
has said it, not even if I have said it, unless it agrees
with your own reason and your own common sense."
—Buddha

THE FIRST BOOK I WROTE ABOUT PARENTING TWINS ADDRESSED
strategies and mindsets for getting through the first year.
The second book dealt with getting through the toddler years.
Not long after my second book was published, people started
asking, "When are you going to write the guide to the preschool
years?" and professing, "I can't wait until you write the guide to
the teen years!"

*Newsflash: Neither is going to happen. I leaned heavily on bakery personnel
and meditation CDs to get through the preschool years, and plan to conveniently
disappear when my oldest turns 13 and reappear when the youngest turns 18.*

After we completed Nina's adoption, numerous well-meaning
friends asked, "When are you going to write a guide on getting
through the adoption process?"

Again, not gonna happen.

It's not that I don't think that all three of those are great book ideas, and would, on some days, be awfully fun to write. I truly hope someone else writes them, and if they do, I promise to buy a copy. However, if I were to write them, my reasons for doing so would be out of line with my spirit.

When I wrote *Ready or Not...Here We Come! The REAL Experts' Guide to the First Year with Twins*, I had one goal and one goal only: to sell it to one person who didn't know me and didn't know someone else who knew me. In other words, a complete and total stranger. That was it. That was my definition of success for that book (clearly, low expectations work for me).

If I were to write a book on preschool-aged twins, teenaged twins, or adoption, the reason I would be doing it was because someone else said that I should. Or because someone else convinced me that I could make good money doing it. Or both.

At the end of the day, if you do anything for either of those reasons alone, you're setting yourself up for disappointment from the get-go. What makes a venture successful, no matter how many outsiders may doubt its potential at the onset, is your passion and desire to do it. If I had woken up each morning and thought, "Ugh, I do *not* want to write this book today, but I will because so-and-so said I should, and hopefully it'll put a few more bucks in the bank," I would have sat down to write with a human brain that was out of sync with its spiritual brain. My train would be off the tracks before leaving the station.

Anything that you do only because you "should" is something you should not be doing! Regardless of the potential payoff, whether financial or emotional, if your heart isn't in it, it won't feel successful because it won't meet *your* definition of success.

We all need to eliminate the word "should" from our vocabulary. Of course, we all have things we have to do. I won't list them because they are obvious, and they'll make you groan. But when you begin to associate nurturing and honoring your spirit with activities that you "should" do, something is out of whack.

When I was finally ready to put pen to paper again, it was because during a drive to Starbucks with my fabulous friend Heather in the front seat and all five screaming children in the back, Heather said, "You have the patience of a saint. I would have lost my mind 15 minutes ago." She then suggested, "You should write a book that lets people in on all your little 'rules.' They obviously keep you pretty sane."

Now *that* intrigued me.

At first, because it sounded completely asinine.

"No one cares about that," I said. "Plus, I don't know how to write about *me*."

"Of course you do," she corrected. "You write about you all the time on your blog, and you love doing it."

Good point.

Over the course of the next few weeks, Heather's idea continued to pop into my head uninvited. The concept became more and more intriguing. Suddenly, with little warning, I found myself bribing the kids with a 67th showing of *High School Musical 2*, and began writing.

From that perspective, if this book sells to only one person who doesn't know me—and doesn't know anyone who knows me—I will deem it successful.

If you're that person, please send me an e-mail.

As women, we often don't acknowledge that we have all the answers we need inside of us. We too often go outside of ourselves—to people we don't know and who don't know us—to get the "right" answer, or to get validation for what we're choosing to do. We lose sight of the fact that we know when we have the "right" answer for us—because it *feels* right. As I like to say, intuition is that moment when your human head and spiritual head are in agreement.

No matter the controversial topic of the moment—to spank or not to spank, to vaccinate on schedule or go with an alternate plan, to fight (or not) for speech therapy for a child who doesn't meet the criteria of "need," but whom a mom simply knows needs assistance—women have varying opinions. Whether or not they'll honestly share those opinions is another story. Which makes it even more dangerous to adopt someone else's "shoulds" while remaining unable to trust one's inner compass.

Most moms struggle with trusting their inner compass—their intuition, their gut instincts—when it comes to their own family and their own children because we are never trained for this job. You want to do surgery on someone? You first need at least ten years of training. You want to put pajamas on an orangutan? Again, many years of training (plus a death wish). But parenting? It's like, "Here's the baby! Best of luck to ya!" We think we know how we feel about everything until we're shoulder-deep in it and those "in the know"—who've actually received all the training—tell us that we're doing it all wrong.

Sometimes, when I speak of intuition, people assume I'm referring to psychic ability. I'm not. Well, maybe I am, a little bit. I'm referring to being psychic with your true self—as in, knowing something "in your gut" without external (and hard) evidence.

One question I often ask myself when I'm struggling to make a decision is, "If I were stranded on a deserted island, what would my decision be?" Regarding the nose piercing, I'd do it in a heartbeat. Regarding spanking, I like to think I'd never do it. Regarding bribery, I'd do it and I'd ask others to bribe me as well. What this tells me is that any choice I may make to the contrary—when *not* on a deserted island—reflects worry over what others might think. Of course, one must occasionally worry about these things. I mean, if you want to tattoo a third eye on your forehead, that might be fine if you're stranded on a deserted island, but I think it's wise to consider how it might affect your day-to-day life around town. If you decide to tattoo a third eye on your forehead with the justification that I somehow said it was okay, by the way, let me be clear that I DIDN'T SAY THAT! In most instances, however, using this approach helps identify what you really want to do versus what you're doing (or not) for "out of whack" reasons.

Another helpful approach is to play the game wherein you ask yourself a question, and then quickly answer with the first thing that comes to mind. The answer that comes out without too much thought is oftentimes the right one for you. Have someone write up a bunch of irrelevant questions such as "What time is it?" "What's your name?" and "Who's your daddy?" and sneak in the question to which you're having trouble coming up with an answer. See what comes out of your mouth without thinking.

Narrowing your personal boundaries is also an important piece of going with your gut. Which is why it's a good idea to make sure to clarify those boundaries as soon as possible.

Every woman has a group of people in her life. It's my belief that each of these people fits into Group A, Group B, or Group C.

Group A is a VIP category. The friends who fit into this group are the ones who know you well, whom you know well, who've got it together enough that you're not always picking up the pieces of their lives that have fallen around them, and who are there for you (and vice versa) whenever necessary. As you go through life, women may come and go from this category, which is completely fine. For example, prior to having kids, Jane, Joyce, and Julie may have been your Group A friends. Perhaps Jane moved to Africa, Julie had quadruplets, and Joyce proclaimed that she wanted to become a nun. Jane may slowly move out of Group A because, while still important to you and a lifelong fixture, she's simply not physically or emotionally present enough to remain in Group A. Ditto for Julie, who fell into the quadruplets' diaper pail and hasn't been heard from since. And Joyce, having entered the nunnery and all, is someone with whom you no longer seem to have much in common. All three women can still be important to you, and you can still vow to be there for them when needed; they're simply no longer your everyday go-to gals.

Most women can count their Group A friends at any point in time on one hand.

Let's skip Group B friends for a moment and discuss Group C friends. Group C friends are the friends and acquaintances who drain you, even if you don't like to admit it. They're sometimes referred to as "energy vampires." They are the folks who always have a problem or a complaint (or both). They seem to come calling when they need help with something, and then swiftly disappear (until the next time). It's not a reciprocal relationship. You're always a giver, rarely (or never) a receiver.

I recently read this quote from G.B. Shaw: "Both optimists and pessimists contribute to society. The optimist invents the airplane, the pessimist the parachute." *Hm*, I thought. *I'm admittedly a nervous flyer. But I prefer to tightly buckle my seatbelt, distract myself with the latest celebrity gossip magazines, and expect a successful landing—not hoist my parachute into the overhead storage bin.* So it makes sense that my Group A friends are going to be those who have the same approach.

It's been said that the quickest way to become who you want to become is to surround yourself with people who are already there. So if you get high off coming up with a solution to every possible problem that comes your way, you'll enjoy the company of like-minded people. If, however, you find that perspective draining, you can group folks who have it into Group C—a.k.a. The Parachute Group.

Finally, there are Group B friends. This group is comprised of those who don't consistently fall into Group A or Group C. For some of these friends, you're more of a giver than a receiver. I honestly think that's okay as long as it's working for you. Some women have an innate need to be needed—to be someone else's Group A friend. Again, as long as it works for you, it's fine. If being someone else's Group A friend ends up draining you more than filling your need to be needed, it's time to move him or her into Group C.

Group B friends are also those whom you genuinely respect, admire, or enjoy, but who aren't around much due either to geographical proximity or lifestyle. I have *many* Group B friends. I'm clear on who's in that category and why. Most women's Group B is large.

Now, on to boundaries. As moms, we have questions. Lots of questions. When we solicit advice, we're opening ourselves up to someone else's opinion. When the person from whom we're soliciting an opinion or suggestion offers it, and vows to love you even if you do exactly the opposite, they're doing their "job" as a friend. If they claim that you're screwing up your kids for life unless you do it their way, they belong in Group C.

I like to think of my boundaries as an invisible force field that surrounds me. When I ask for advice, the force field is down so that I can receive it. When advice is given to me unsolicited, the force field is up so that I can repel it if necessary. It's kind of like that saying kids use: "I'm rubber and you're glue. What you say bounces off of me and sticks to you."

If you believe in, say, bribery and utilize it in the checkout line, and the stranger behind you chastises you because of it, you simply have to have your boundary force field activated such that you may hear her words, but are not affected by them. You don't collapse in a heap, either questioning your parenting approach or crying hysterically because someone disapproved of it (or both).

Advice and flat-out instruction will come at you from every direction once you become a mom. Every person thinks his or her way is the best way. And each of them is right. Their way *is* the best way—*for them*. It's simply arrogant to assume that it's best for anyone else. And the very fact that someone offers unsolicited advice quite possibly indicates that they aren't completely comfortable with what they're doing as a parent. In many cases, they want others to get on their bandwagon so that they are more comfortable with their choices. Does that make sense?

So, practice having an active force field around you when necessary. Advice, subtle or otherwise, will come from everywhere— strangers, friends, and family alike. Thank people for their interest, smile, move on, and do your own thing.

Rule 14
Aging: It's All the Rage

—◆—

"Wrinkles should merely indicate
where smiles have been."
—Mark Twain

THE OTHER DAY WHILE RIDING IN THE CAR, GRACE TURNED TO me and asked, "Mom, when you were my age, was the United States still 13 colonies?"

"I refuse to justify that question with an answer," I responded.

Not long before that, The Senator stated, "Mom, when Grandpa Bill was growing up, all these mountains were volcanoes, you know. They've been quiet for a long time."

Grandpa Bill was thrilled.

Last fall, The Beach Boys played a concert in our neighborhood. After the conclusion of "Kokomo," Heather's husband Michael asked Henry, "What do you think of the band? They're pretty good, huh?"

Henry's response: "Yeah. But why are they so old?"

Ah, yes. Our age is, to our kids anyway, decrepit.

I understand their perspective, frankly. I mean, at what point did *you* notice that your doctors are all younger than you? It's bad.

I wanted to scream even louder after I made a mid-contraction comment to my obstetrician about *The Electric Company* and she hadn't a clue what I was talking about.

But hey, we're as old as we feel, right? David claims he's in better health mentally and physically than he was in his twenties. I believe him. And when I turn forty, if I look like Demi Moore, Courtney Cox, or Julia Roberts, I promise to be utterly and completely thrilled with the aging process.

In an effort to continue to at least *feel* younger, I recently bought a jogging stroller. And not for the first time.

Shortly after Jack and Henry were born, I bought my first jogging stroller. I was 110% sure that I would run with those babies (even though I'd run only once in my life prior, and it was to keep my 2-year-old from pulling a display of oranges so beautiful it looked fake onto herself in the grocery store).

I was determined to lose the pregnancy weight, stay energetic enough to survive the craziness, and have a valid excuse to escape the house the moment it came time to load the dishwasher each evening.

Apparently, the early onset sleep deprivation brought on by caring for newborn twins who were on opposite every-other-hour feeding schedules (leaving us with a baby who needed to be fed every hour around the clock) affected my decision-making skills.

The running never happened. A few years later, after stubbornly admitting defeat, a wonderful new mom of twins in Illinois got a smoking deal on a three-year-old, twice-used, double jogging stroller.

The second time around, however, I was 111% sure I would run. Dr. Oz says we ought to engage in activities that keep our hearts healthy. And I'd walk a tightrope across the Grand Canyon in a thong if Dr. Oz thought it was good for my health. Plus, I'm still trying to lose a few pounds (from the pregnancy that produced the now 5-year-old).

Anyway, Heather bought a jogging stroller, and was anxiously touting the value of running in the desert—before the sun comes up—enjoying the relative quiet, and the quail, and the quarry blasting that goes on two miles north. In theory, it sounded like a great idea. Heather was in love with her stroller—even though it was still in the box—and so I hit the store hoping to buy the exact same one. So that we could look like complete dorks trying to fight aging together.

As I attempted to assemble both Heather's and my stroller in my living room, I was thrilled with my decision to get exactly the same model she'd purchased, as it made assembly awfully easy. Except for a minor inconvenience. Or two. My brake and pedometer were broken.

Of course.

Because seriously, every time I buy an assembly-required product, a piece is missing. Or broken. I swear, I'm cursed.

I meticulously inspect all boxes before purchasing to ensure that no one has attempted to open them since they left their manufacturer. There could be 28 boxes on the shelf, and even after reaching *waaaaaay* to the back to claim an untouched one, there's an issue. It's inevitable. And I've simply come to accept that, in all likelihood, I chronically forgot to insert one or two pieces of a product into its box before returning it in a prior life, and so it's my karma catching up with me.

The next morning I took Nina and George (whom I often refer to as Diego, of *Go, Diego, Go* fame because there was a time when George was convinced he *was* Diego and would not respond unless you addressed him as such), with me for my first run. It was awesome. And by awesome, I mean just okay.

But, as with other less-than-fun experiences, one must often turn to her sense of humor (assuming she has one) to survive.

Adopting that approach allowed me to glean a few tricks—between episodes of hyperventilation—that make running palatable for women who, like myself, abhor running.

And in fact, these tricks, when applied properly, can make nearly any painful situation more enjoyable.

First, if we're talking about buying a jogging stroller to keep our real age a few years younger than our chronological age, buy one that has built-in speakers. It's hard to hate life too much when good music's playing. If you, like me, hate having ear buds fall out of you ears and the wire that connects them to the mp3 player wrap around you in a way that makes you jog like *Friends'* Phoebe Buffay to avoid tripping, the built-in speakers are for you. Now, I've not yet figured out why the speakers face my daughter and not me but, as Heather says, beggars can't be choosers. Not that I was begging to jog, but I think you know what I mean.

Even if we're not talking about jogging, no matter what less-than-enjoyable task you're going to engage in, make sure you have good music with you. I think this is why I see so many people grocery shopping with iPods these days. Smart, smart women.

Second (we're back to running), if you're as lucky as I am to have a commercialized area in your neighborhood, when you start to feel like you're overheating (meaning that your body temperature has surpassed 99.2), holler to the kid on the Go, Diego, Go bike—who's continuing to shout over his shoulder, "Mom, can you please hurry up!"—and request, "Diego, hold up; I need to stop at the market!"

Proceed directly to the refrigerated aisle. Don't worry about the deli guy who has a look in his eye that asks, "Should I call 9-1-1?" Realize it's just because you look fantastic; you're sweating, and hyperventilating, and leaning over the stroller's handlebar while possibly drooling. Wipe your brow (and your mouth) and keep going.

Do not be distracted when your child asks what you'll be buying him. Don't be tempted when he asks for a donut. But if they have donut samples available, grab one.

You want a donut now, don't you. Sorry.

If you're not running, but instead driving, find a drive-thru Starbucks. Or an In-n-Out Burger. Or a Krispy Kreme (are there *any* Krispy Kremes left?). Or some establishment that was forward thinking enough to build a drive-thru and has something that will cool you off, warm you up, or otherwise give you an *Ahhhhhh* moment.

After a few minutes in the refrigerated section of our local market, I felt refreshed and announced it was time to leave. Diego was totally ecstatic and let everyone know on his way out how happy he was to be leaving without a maple-glazed bismark.

We crossed Main Street and began to make our way home. It was at that point that I noticed we were approaching a slight incline.

"Diego?" I inquired. "Do you know CPR?"

"You're going to buy me a guitar?" he responded.

Never mind.

In a second-wave effort to channel a smidge of Demi's *G.I. Jane* appearance when I begin my fifth decade, I invited Grace on a Rollerblading jaunt one Saturday morning.

Truth be told, I'm not a very good Rollerblader. In fact, I really stink. I simply cannot get the hang of braking. Look, at heart, I'm a roller *skater*. I prefer to stop by dragging my pointed toe behind me. And couples skate? With your comb in your back pocket and your index finger laced through your partner's belt loop? Please.

I bought new Rollerblades because I was completely sure that all my technical blading issues arose from an old brake (David and

I bought our rollerblades in 1996. It's true that I've only used them twice since then. But they're still old.)

But then Grace put on the archaic Rollerblades, flew at mach speed down the street, and stopped on a dime.

Nice.

My new blades are really pretty. They're green. And shiny. And my bright blue sparkly helmet? Let me tell ya, the heads of *all* the construction workers turn when I roll by wearing it and shouting "Whoa! Whoa!" with arms flailing.

As I mentioned, Grace Rollerblades really fast. Sometimes I think she's showing off. Like when she was two and she'd waddle into the kitchen and declare, "Mama, 'puter's bootin' up."

I taught the kid how to boot up the computer. I taught her how to ride a bike. But clearly, in the area of Rollerblading, it was I who was to be schooled.

"Mom, this is so easy," she insisted. "Just put your head down and go."

Mm-hm.

I chose to head to a section of our neighborhood that is barely inhabited. Just us and the road and my huge learning curve.

And a steep hill.

Up we went. Huffing and puffing and "giving it hell," as Heather would say.

"Mom, what is the deal? Can you not go *any faster?*" asked Grace, as though she were late for a meeting with Joe Jonas.

"Please…Hold…Coming," was all I could utter between attempts to intake oxygen.

Once we reached the top, the view was fantastic. The city skyline, the smog and pollution settling in the valley; it was awesome.

Except that what goes up must come down.

"Grace, honestly, this is terrifying," I admitted as I stood at the precipice. And what was so terrifying? You guessed it: my braking inability.

"Mom," she hollered whizzing down the hill 30 feet (and growing) in front of me, "It's great! Just go for it!"

"GRACE!" I hollered, hands cupping either side of my mouth, "SLOW DOWN! NOT IN THE MOOD FOR THE EMERGENCY ROOM TODAY!"

"Mom, it's great! Just remember, feel the wind, not the concrete!" she encouraged, flying farther and farther in front of me.

Good advice.

Her sing-song voice trailed off (she was still talking about something, likely *Twilight*—or Joe Jonas—related, reminding me of the 80's Peppermint Patty commercial wherein some lady touts "the extra cool sensation of gale force winds whipping through my haaaaaaiiiiiiiir!" Remember that?).

I finally made it to the bottom of the hill, where Grace was casually perched on the corner of the sidewalk.

"Mom, I've been here, like, forever. It's been two minutes and nine seconds—*just* since you came into sight."

"Did my best, Grace. Didn't wanna die."

Suddenly, without warning, there it was. The O'mighty eye roll. Otherwise known as the pre-tween girl's calling card.

I suppose it would be wise to be grateful that she waited for me. Somehow, I'm sure we're only days shy of her not acknowledging she knows me. When that day comes, I'll come flying down the hill screaming, completely out of control, and a classmate biking by will ask, "Is that your Mom?"

"Who? What?"

I can't wait.

Another way in which kids can make us feel older than the moon is by subtly yet constantly reminding us how quickly technology is advancing.

When I was in college (which was not that long ago), cell phones were big as a brick and came with a "tower" you had to somehow magnetize to the top of your car during the few moments when you wanted to make a call. (I don't know the exact way in which they worked because I didn't have one; the entire setup cost, I believe, an arm and a leg.)

As you are likely aware, we've come awfully far technologically since yesteryear.

No one is more aware of this than a 10-year-old who has not yet been blessed with a cell phone to call her own.

After I made my own technological leap to a BlackBerry not that long ago, I had my old phone's plan altered so that it could be the kids' phone. The intent was for it to be available to them were they to have an after-school event or a birthday party and need to contact me in a covert way.

I presented the phone to Grace one evening so that I could show her how to use it.

"Okay, now Grace, here's what you do," I began.

"Mom, I don't need instructions. I get it," she replied (after the obligatory eye roll).

"Okay, but…"

"Mom, just let me check it out. If I have questions, I'll ask."

Two minutes later our home phone rang.

"Could someone get that?" I asked.

"Don't worry, Mom; it's me," announced Grace. "I'm just practicing."

30 seconds later my cell phone rang.

"Hello?"

"What's up?"

"Hello Grace. I think you've got the hang of it. Could you turn off the phone and put it in your backpack now?"

"Yes, after I take a picture of the dog for the screensaver."

"Honey, there's no camera on that phone."

"Yes, there is. I'm using it now."

Really?

"Also, can I take some video?"

"I *know* there's not video on there."

"Yes, there is. I'm using it now."

I missed out on so much!

My phone again began ringing.

"GRACE!"

"Okay, okay, I'm putting it away. But about texting…" she inquired.

I waited until the next morning to break it to her that, while I'm sure the phone *can* text, *she* cannot. Because I don't yet know how to, myself.

We can't stop ourselves from getting older. Don't think of it as getting older; think of it as getting wiser.

There is a book that I've seen several times in the J. Jill store called *Wise Women: A Celebration of Their Insights, Courage, and Beauty*, by Joyce Tenneson. It contains photographs of wise women, several of whom have reached their hundredth birthday.

Sure, they have wrinkles. And some of them are the most beautiful women I've ever seen. Each wrinkle tells a story. Each wrinkle is the result of a hundred thousand smiles.

I remember the *Oprah* segment that explored the Blue Zones—areas of the world where people live longer than anywhere else. Loma Linda, California, is the only Blue Zone in the United States. Dr. Oz interviewed several people in this community. They interviewed a 94-year-old surgeon named Ellsworth Wareham who still performs open-heart surgery on a daily basis. I'll never forget Marge, who at 103 years young has a daily exercise routine that includes a seven- to eight-mile ride on a stationary bike followed by weight lifting. At one point in the middle of her weight-lifting routine, Dr. Oz assumed she was finished. She was quick to inform him, "I'm not done yet!" I hope and intend to be Marge.

We age. It's a fact of life. It doesn't help that technology advances more quickly than we do and makes some of us *feel* older with the release of each new iPhone app we can't figure out how to download.

I try not to get bent out of shape over every new gray hair or stray line. I just head to the store for some hair spray paint or eye cream. And try not to look into the mirror that often. Or, I treat myself to a facial, claiming medical necessity.

I figure we can't stop it, so we might as well go with it.

Rule 15
Keep Your Eyes on the Prize

———— ⊷ ————

"The art of being wise is the art of
knowing what to overlook."
—William James

I OCCASIONALLY HAVE TO WORK HARD TO REMAIN CALM ON DAYS
when I'm demonstratively loved a wee bit less than David (who
spends all day *not* cooking meals, driving to and from soccer practice, buying clothing he isn't in love with but is willing to live with
because his *child* is in love with it, and enduring viewing after viewing of the same *Veggie Tales* movie).

George spent the first three years of his life on my hip
like an interesting fashion accessory. But the second he blew out
those four candles, he took to running down the street after my
husband hollering, "Bye, Papa, I LOVE YOU!" until David's truck
had been out of sight for at least eight minutes. One day, he ended
a monotony-breaking trip to Target yelling at the top of his lungs,
"Papa! *Papaaaaa!*" as I encouraged him toward the exit while smiling at the nervous onlookers and wondering what exactly it might
take to win this kid over.

My last Mother's Day began exactly as expected. A beautiful

tray of freshly washed strawberries, a tower of made-from-scratch pancakes smothered in organic butter and pure Vermont maple syrup, a steaming mug of Ethiopian coffee. The final touch? One single red gerbera daisy in a tall, skinny, vintage vase. It was magic.

It was also the tail end of the dream from which I was rudely awakened.

"Get off of me!" "You touched my toe!" "I HATE YOUR KNEECAP!"

And the all-too-familiar sound of my husband snoring through it all.

Up I jumped from bed, starving, to retrieve the smiling 1-year-old from her crib.

"Papa Papa Papa," she greeted.

Hm.

Out to the family room I sauntered with Nina on my hip.

"Happy Mother's Day, Mom!" welcomed Big Daddy.

"Well, thank you, Jack! I wasn't sure anyone had remembered."

In walked Grace, Henry, and George in slow succession. They plopped onto the couch, after arguing for a moment about who would sit where.

"Mom, what's for breakfast?" moaned Grace.

"Yeah, I want cereal *and* pancakes," declared George.

"Get OFF of me," shouted Henry, who was sitting alone.

"Did everyone forget what day it is today?" asked Big Daddy.

"Is it Christmas?" asked George, running to find his stocking.

I sank into my chair in the family room with Humphrey, the only non-housetrained 2-year-old Cockapoo in history, and the only family member who is hugely attached to me for a reason no more profound than undying, unconditional love. I wouldn't have been surprised if he made me a card. I anxiously awaited its arrival.

Finally, David emerged from his slumber.

"Okay, everyone, it's Sunday. Do you know what that means?" he asked.

I waited on the edge of my less-than-comfortable chair for the sound of heralding trumpets and a proclamation that it was my day and everyone needed to bid me *adieu* as I headed to the nearest spa.

"It's cleaning day!" he announced with the same level of enthusiasm with which I fantasized the aforementioned announcement being delivered.

"But...it's Mother's Day!" countered Big Daddy, as though that gave both mom *and* him a free ride.

"We also need to put laundry away," reminded David.

"But...it's MOTHER'S DAY!" hollered Henry. "We don't have to do *anything* on Mother's Day!"

And then, in a moment of what can only be described as the sweetest, purest love on the planet, George sauntered up to David, wrapped his arms tightly around his leg, squeezed, and in the most angelic voice you can imagine, said...wait for it..."Happy Mother's Day, Daddy."

One year, just before Christmas, the doorbell rang on a chaotic Saturday afternoon. Everyone went running as though Santa himself had arrived. I understood; there's not much excitement around here. So when the doorbell rings, the very idea of just who it could be is enough to get any of the kids up from their Wii marathon for a moment or two.

Not Santa. Just the Santa-hat-wearing UPS man delivering two boxes.

When I brought them in, the kids asked in unison, "What is that? Who is that for? Is it a treehouse? Or a pony?"

"They're Christmas presents," I answered flatly.

"For who?" Jack asked.

"Whom," I corrected.

"Huh?"

"Nothing. They're for nice people."

"Nice people?" Jack asked.

"Yeah. You know, people who are nice to me. Those are the people who'll get the presents."

"Well, shoot. Guys, don't get excited," he screamed to his siblings. "The presents are for Michael and Heather."

Over the years I've determined that it's in my best interest to create my own place in the world where I'm not defined by being needed (or, on some days, even liked) by my kids. Because one day, God willing, they are going to grow up and do their own thing. And while I will miss them terribly, this ultimate independence *is* what we hope for as parents, right? Because the way I see it, if I have a 35-year-old lying on my couch asking me to make him a PB&J sandwich and wondering when his laundry will be done, something has gone horribly awry.

When our kids are young, we want them to appreciate all that we do for them. But we also must remember how important it is for us to teach them to become independent from us.

As Joyce Maynard so eloquently stated, "It's not only children who grow. Parents do too. As much as we watch to see what our children do with their lives, they are watching us to see what we do with ours. I can't tell my children to reach for the sun. All I can do is reach for it, myself."

Rule 16
Give Yourself the Little Blue Box

⸺⸱⋖∞⋗⸱⸺

"I don't like myself. I'm crazy about myself."
—Mae West

O N JACK'S AND HENRY'S SEVENTH BIRTHDAY, I LAZILY LAY IN
our less-than-optimally-comfortable hotel bed and relived
their delivery in my mind (which isn't the most pleasant of memories, frankly. Worth it, but not terribly pleasant).

Suddenly, someone with a very loud voice began poking me and
shouting, "GRACE! GRACE! WHERE IS JACK?"

"Henry," I answered, "he and Papa went to pick up breakfast.
I'm sleeping. And I'm not Grace."

He trotted back into the hotel room's living area and opened the
door to the hallway over and over hoping to catch a glimpse of his
brother, undoubtedly to scream to him that it was their birthday
(in case Jack didn't know).

I called him back into the bedroom and enthusiastically proclaimed, "Henry, Happy Birthday!"

"Happy Birthday," he sullenly responded.

"Henry, it's *your* birthday. You don't have to wish *me*
Happy Birthday."

"I wasn't," he clarified, sounding just like Senator Eeyore. "I was wishing myself a happy birthday."

This made me laugh. It also taught me a lesson. Sometimes we wait for others to give us what we want or need. But one, we aren't clear about what that is. And two, sometimes we have to be our own best friend.

There was a time when I thought the little blue box from Tiffany's was love made manifest. I waited and waited and waited for it to be presented to me. It never appeared. I'll admit that I spent some time feeling sure that this meant that David didn't love me.

And then one day, I proactively ended my pity party and waltzed into Tiffany's. I made nice with Margaret, the bejeweled lady behind the counter, and told her, "Margaret, I need a blue box. I've been waiting to receive one for years, and it appears it isn't going to happen unless I do it myself." She nodded in complete understanding, as though she'd heard this song many times before, and handed me the smallest blue box under the counter.

I went home, put my engagement ring in it, put it on my pillow, and gave an Oscar-winning performance to the stuffed animals that lay strewn about our bedroom when I "discovered" and opened it later that evening.

The fact is, we must tell other people what we want and need. Dr. Phil is notorious for admonishing that we must teach other people how to treat us. Don't waste time being a martyr in order to get what you need. Doing so assumes that others don't want to give you what you need, and it makes it harder on everyone.

Relying on others to fulfill your needs takes far more energy than most of us have. I give myself a birthday present each year. Or I flat-out tell David that I want this book or that blanket.

Alice Roosevelt Longworth perfectly summed up my perspective. She said, "I have a simple philosophy. Fill what's empty. Empty what's full. Scratch where it itches." If I need a girls-day-out, I don't beat around the bush, hoping for someone to take the hint and then try to hit the nail on the head in terms of exactly how what I'm hoping to be asked to do. I call a girlfriend and say, "I need a day out. When are you available?" It's the quickest path to getting what I need. Which is fantastic, because I don't have a lot of extra time on my hands.

Rule 17
Expect Misunderstandings

⸺⟨∞⟩⸺

"Confusion now hath made his masterpiece."
—William Shakespeare

ONE DAY, ON A WHIM, I BOUGHT THE KIDS TWO GOLDFISH. YOU already know where this story is going, don't you?

Here was my logic: 12 cents per fish plus $5.99 for a mighty cool bowl equals 27 minutes of peace and quiet as the kids argue over what to name the coolest pets since Grace was allowed to buy the hamster she claimed she couldn't live without (but then proceeded not to care too much about until she found him motionless and cold one sunny afternoon).

Final choice for the fishes' birth certificates: Wanda and Cosmo—apparently the names of characters from *The Fairly Oddparents*.

The kids were most disappointed when I consistently referred to their precious fish as Wilma and Carlos. In my defense, I couldn't remember their actual names as *The Fairly Oddparents* runs a close second to *SpongeBob* as Mom's Least Favorite Show Ever.

A week or so later, as I was painstakingly baking bread (don't ask), Grace stopped mid-monologue to ask with a surprising lack of emotion, "Mom, why is Cosmo lying at the bottom of the bowl?"

"Probably because he's dead," I responded. I was completely kidding. Self-fulfilling prophecies can really bite you on the you-know-what.

Grace called everyone inside. They engaged for several minutes in less-than-friendly banter about how Cosmo might have died. Specifically, it seemed critical to ascertain whose fault it was.

"You forgot to feed him," accused Big Daddy.

"That's not true," retorted Henry. "I fed him, like, seven times."

"This morning?" I inquired.

"Well—" responded Henry incredulously. "He said he was really hungry!"

With that, the powder room funeral commenced. Grace asked everyone to bow their heads in prayer. George asked us to repeat his Montessori prayer after him, line by line—his Montessori prayer, which, at one point, includes the line, "I feel your pain."

"I feel my pain," I repeated, as instructed, after George.

The world stood still.

"No, Mom," corrected George. "I feel *your* pain."

"You do?" I asked.

George froze in confusion.

Cosmo, Carlos, whoever you are, I hope you are resting in peace with the knowledge that we will try to take good care of our sole fish called Wanda.

It happens to the best of us. The child who is normally happier than a pig in mud has a day when her sweet little disposition heads south. I wasn't sure why, but by 10:00 the morning of a historic event known as The Nosedive of Nina's Angelic Nature, I was convinced she had an ear infection.

I called the pediatrician to make an appointment.

Now, when you have five children, making a last-minute appointment with a pediatrician is harder than you might imagine. The call goes something like this.

"Hi. I need an appointment because blah blah blah. Keep in mind, however, that I'm 45 minutes away, and my older kids get out of school at 2:45, so I have to be out of your office by 2:00—better make it 1:45 in case of traffic—or I could come sometime after 3:30, but then I have to be out of there by 4:30 because two of my older kids have Tae Kwon Do, and at the rate I pay for them both to participate, they may not miss a session unless they are hospitalized.

"Yes, my daughter's name is Nina. Oh, but for insurance purposes you'll have to put Rahel. Why? Well, Nina's not the name on her birth certificate. Did we decide we didn't like her name? No. It's sort of convoluted. Familiar with international adoption? No? Okay, just put Rahel on everything and we'll work it out later. She's not in the system? That's weird. David said he called. Oh, you have a Nina born on April 19? No, I'm bringing a Rahel born on April 20. Again, long story. Yes, I'm sure this kid is mine. And yes, right now it is very much all about me."

Twenty minutes into our drive to the doctor with George in the back complaining that whatever was on satellite TV wasn't what he wanted (again), I suddenly realized (after considering how naive I was for believing that satellite TV would save my life), *Uh oh, I had an interview twelve minutes ago for an article in Pregnancy magazine. Hm.*

But "Hm" isn't what came out of my mouth so I guess that satellite TV and its accompanying headphones came in handy after all.

Honestly, it was an insane week in general. The big kids had started school on Monday so they were exhausted beyond reason. Henry claimed his teacher told him that he and he alone was exempt from homework all year long. Grace wanted to have a play-date every afternoon. And I was again subsisting on handfuls of Craisins and four non-consecutive hours of sleep per night.

At some point during the previous few months, I decided to plant maiden grass alongside our front walk. As I've mentioned, we live in the desert. And I had simply grown tired of looking at plants that were, in fact, little more than a few leaves struggling to survive until lunchtime while holding on for dear life to a whole mess of barren sticks posing as their host.

I anticipated that on days when the thermometer climbs dangerously close to its maximum reading of 120 degrees, I would derive great joy from looking out my front door and being reminded of the northeast—not that I've ever lived in the northeast, but I am quite certain that it is a place where, in mid-July, folks glide through town on old-fashioned bicycles, their wicker baskets cuddling loaves of freshly baked French bread and containers of wild, organic (not to mention free) raspberries.

So I bought and planted maiden grass. All to convince myself that I'm not in the desert and it never hits 120 degrees. A most wise investment, if I do say so.

After only a few months in our yard, the maiden grass was thriving like nothing should in the desert. Maybe it's because I named them all. I greet Dasher, Dancer, Prancer, Vixen, Comet, Cupid, Donder, Blitzen, and Maria each morning, and profusely apologize for the yelling they've endured as it wafted through the airtight but not soundproof windows of our home over the previous 24 hours.

As I approached the walkway after a long day of dropping off, picking up, dropping off, picking up, and talking myself down from ten or eleven ledges, I noticed a change in my maiden grass.

"Geez, these things have grown two feet!" I exclaimed.

"Where?" asked George.

"Right here. These grasses have grown two feet."

"I don't see them," replied George, his confusion escalating as he bent in half to inspect the bottoms of the plants for toes.

I quickly remembered how literal 4-year-olds are, just as George announced, "Oh, I see them!"

Now I was the confused party.

However, upon further inspection, I realized that sometimes, in the creative and flexible mind of a 4-year-old, reality is—at any given moment—whatever one declares it to be, as the maiden grass had, indeed, grown two feet.

To fulfill the second-grade homework requirement of twenty minutes per night of at-home reading, Henry began devouring the *Harry Potter* series.

"Professor McDougal saw—" started Henry.

"McGonagall," I corrected.

"Oh," said Henry. "It's a hard word to announce."

"Pronounce."

"Dad, this is so mean," continued Henry, obviously ignoring me. "Listen to this. 'Harry had a thin face, knobbly knees, black hair, and bright green eyes. He wore round glasses held together with a lot of Scotch tape because of all the times Dudley had punched him on the nose.'"

"Is he bleeding?" asked George.

"NO GEORGE," responded Henry, angrily. "THIS IS A BOOK! IT'S NOT REAL!"

At that moment, Jack ran in the front door with his remote control dragonfly. "This thing is out of juice," he announced.

"*I* want some juice!" expressed George.

"No, he means—" I attempted to explain.

"But I WANT SOME JUICE!" reiterated George.

"George," I calmly stated, "We're not having juice."

"But Jack is!" hollered George. "Jack, you're going to be on the naughty list."

"No I'm *not*, George!" replied Jack. "My dragonfly is out of batteries!"

"Professor McDoogal—" continued Henry.

"McGonagall," I corrected.

"Whoever," Henry conceded.

"JUUUIIIIICE!!!!" yelled George.

Be prepared for the fact that misunderstandings won't solely involve folks under the age of ten.

Ralph is the 80-year-old barista at our local grocery store's Starbucks. I can't grocery shop without a latte in hand, and at one point, I happened to have a gift card that allowed me between 15 and 20 lattes, depending on their size and whether or not I felt the need for whip on any particular day.

When Ralph scanned my Starbucks card and saw that I had $47 left, he said, "Wow! Nice gift card!"

"Yes," I replied. "From my fantastic peeps."

I think I lost him.

"You know," he continued, "The only thing better than using a gift card to buy yourself a coffee is—"

I seriously thought he was going to ask me to buy *him* a coffee. He should have. I would have told him to make it a venti *and* add whip.

He pulled out a gift tin of Ethiopian coffee.

"This precious gift tin of Ethiopian coffee is rare. It has sundried cherries in it."

"Is that good, Ralph? Coffee with sundried cherries?"

"Well, ma'am, I don't know. But it sounds good. *And* it's 20%

off—today only."

"Wow!" I replied. "So how much does that make that fine tin of Ethiopian coffee with sundried cherries?"

"Well, *today only*," he reiterated, "just $10!"

"Well, Ralph, that is most interesting," I noted. "You see, my daughter was born in Ethiopia."

"Really?" asked Ralph. "That *is* most interesting."

"I'll take it, Ralph. You're a good salesman. Wrap it up!" I requested.

He leaned *waaaaaay* over so as to better see the card reader as he swiped my debit card, and as he waited for the receipt to print, he glanced up—with eyes the same shade of blue as Luigi the Plumber's—and looked toward Grace.

"You mean that she was born in Ethiopia?"

"No, she was born in Illinois. My other daughter was born in Ethiopia."

"Oh, wow!" he exclaimed, slowly bringing himself to an upright position. "So…what happened? Were you on safari or something?"

I paused. And then, I'm sorry, and I realize I'm probably going to hell for this, but I couldn't resist.

"Yes, Ralph, I was on safari and right there in the bush I had to hop off my elephant and deliver a child."

His eyes got as wide as prize-winning watermelons at the state fair.

"I'm kidding, Ralph. She was adopted."

"Oh!" You could see him visibly deflate with relief.

I'm going to divulge information sure to win me Under-Parenter of the Year. I don't sit at the breakfast table engaged in conversation with the kids in the morning. My pediatrician might chastise me, yet somehow I doubt she does it with regularity either.

The way I do spend my mornings is thus: standing like a cheer-leader in the middle of the kitchen (or while running from kitch-en to laundry room to office to bathroom) directing people to "finish eating," "stop talking," "get off the dog," and "bring me your folder for god's sake so I can sign it *once* this week." And not necessarily in that order.

One morning, Jack was paying little-to-no attention to my re-quests to bring me his folder because he was too busy talking about how he got invited to a friend's birthday party but Henry didn't because only Jack's class was invited.

Here is the conversation that ensued when I was close to my breaking point.

"Jack, if you can't bring me your folder, I can't call your friend's mom and let her know that you'll be coming to his birthday party."

"Well," responded Jack, "You can't call his mom anyway."

"Why not?"

"He doesn't have a mom. He has two dads."

"Okay, that's fine," I said. "Just don't tell Sarah Palin."

"He has two Dads?" asked Henry, as casually as one might ask what day it is.

I had barely opened my mouth to respond when Jack asked, "Who's Sarah Painting?"

And the ping pong ball bounced to Henry who responded with, "Sarah's painting what?"

I instinctively put my index finger up, as though they gave a hoot what I had to say on the matter, but then thought better of it and simply went about my business making lunch times three, remembering all the while that while I did not grow up in times when having two dads or two moms was typical, in this day and age it's not what I would call *atypical*. I gave thanks for our children who are unfazed by it, and for the fact that they didn't ask me—

that morning anyway—how two dads go about having a baby.

Misunderstandings abound while parenting, which is why I en-joy following Rule 18.

Rule 18
Keep One Ear Open at All Times

---

*"There is no such thing as a worthless conversation,
provided you know what to listen for."*
—James Nathan Miller

A
S MOMS, WE'RE SO USED TO THE SCREAMING AND TATTLING
that it's natural to occasionally tune out when our kids talk.
Which is why moms occasionally find art drawn all over the dining
room walls. Which the kids insist that mom said was okay. What
actually happened was, in a moment of parental exhaustion, a kid
said, "Can I color blah blah blah?" Mom was too tired to have
clearly heard anything after the word "color" and responded,
"Whatever," at which point freestyle art commenced. While occasionally messy, I understand and fully support the tuning-out
approach because it's been known to keep me from flipping out.
In places like The Gap.

I've learned, however, that sometimes the best therapy is to
pay attention while *pretending* to be tuning out. *Especially* when
they think you're not listening (and, therefore, not trying to get
your attention with a report on who's thinking about looking at
whose ankle the wrong way), kids' comments and philosophical

analyses of life can be downright hilarious gems you'll treasure for a lifetime.

One afternoon, we were in the car on our way home from school. One of Jack's eight girlfriends (one for every year of his life) had moved out of the area the week prior. Jack was telling Grace about this massive upheaval in his world—a scenario made more hysterical by the fact that Grace had on headphones and was looking out the window. Jack confided, "Paisley's gone. I'm just a wreck!"

One morning a few months after our fifth child came along, I was in my bathroom trying to decide between blue and brown ponytail holders when I overheard George talking to David with great enthusiasm.

"Dad," he said, "I have a 'portant question to ask. When Mom and I go to Target today, can we buy Cinnamon Toast Crunch?"

"Um, Mom is taking you. Why don't you ask her?" responded David.

My thoughts exactly; David and I are so in tune.

"Because she'll say 'No'," sulked George. "'Cause it has too much sugar."

"Well, dude, it does. So the answer is probably 'No'," informed David.

George thought for a second or two.

"Dad…well…first of all, don't call me 'Dude'. Also, can we get Cinnamon Toast Crunch when mom has another baby in her belly?"

I didn't see or hear from David for days.

One day after school, Henry got into Lulu and commented that he'd had the best day ever. Naturally, I was intrigued.

"What was so great about it?" asked Jack.

"Remember, we learned about the human bladder?"

Not "the bladder," but "the *human* bladder," as though it is somehow different in form and function from the tiger bladder, the dog bladder, and the ape bladder (but what do I know, maybe it is).

Henry then sat in the back seat talking about the (human) bladder for at least an hour. Unbeknownst to him, I know more about the human bladder than do most urologists. It was quite enlightening.

Most mornings in our household, cereal is served with a large side order of "Move over!" "You're too close to me!" "You smell!" and "Leave me alone!"

One day, as Henry sat down next to George, David and I grabbed the kitchen counter, bracing ourselves for the onslaught of opposition. Instead, George said, "Thank you for sitting next to me, my sweet love!"

After multiple attempts to enter his pre-tween sister's room—after she'd told him "No" 13 times—George's finger was sadly the thing that received her message as the door and door frame made a sandwich out of it.

For reasons I have yet to comprehend, Jack and Henry said they'd be his servants after this event. The very idea of this immediately eased George's pain, and from the comfort of my office, the dialogue I could overhear immediately eased all my frustration over a computer that refused to reboot.

"Do you want something to drink?" asked Jack.

"Yes," answered George, suddenly more perky, with a hint of morose for effect. "And a sandwich might make me feel better, too."

"What kind?" asked Jack.

"Ummmmm, I'll have peanut butter and honey. BUT with the peanut butter spread EVERYwhere and the honey only in dots on top of the peanut butter…six dots…and no crust."

"Okaaaaay? Well, it's kind of hard to put dots of honey on there."

"Well, just try," encouraged George.

Jack then aged 28 years and insisted, "You need to have some fruit."

"How about strawberries?" asked George, becoming cheerier with each addition to the menu.

"We don't have strawberries. We have bananas and blueberries and grapes."

"Well, I don't like *any* of those things," stated George with disgust.

"Dude, I can't find peanut butter. You're going to have to have honey and jelly."

At this point, Henry (who had actually suggested the whole servitude thing but then remained on the Henry-sized couch indentation with Wii remote in hand, intently focused on expeditiously getting SpongeBob to some place in Crusty Crab-land) emerged from his Wii Trance long enough to proclaim, "Um, that's just gross."

"He likes it!" declared Jack.

"Yeah, I like it," confirmed George.

"Here it is, George!"

With great pride, Jack presented George with his creation.

To which George responded, "Uh, there's a piece of crust on there."

"Well, pull it off then!" retorted Jack, clearly becoming a wee bit annoyed.

"You do it. My finger hurts," demanded George, taking his role as the injured 4-year-old in great need a tish too far.

Somewhat surprisingly, however, Jack rolled his eyes and graciously accommodated George's request.

"Thanks," uttered an again-perky George. "I'd also like some chips. And I'd like to watch *The Jonas Brothers* but my finger hurts so you have to change the channel."

Ah, the sweet, sweet opportunity to enjoy this exchange from the comfort of the couch-turned-desk in the living room, as opposed to my normal perspective. After a few minutes, I decided to pretend to smash my finger in a door. I was hungry.

I've found that the most innocent, hilarious, memory-worthy utterances can happen when the kids think I'm not paying attention. Keeping an ear open has also allowed me to learn just how easy it is to love the simple things, as I detail in Rule 25. So when I really need a good laugh—or a new perspective-altering mantra—I simply grab a notebook and a bag of chips, and plant myself in a good hiding spot within earshot of their current conversation.

Rule 19
Be Prepared for Difficult Questions

⸺◦∞◦⸺

"A child can ask questions that a wise man cannot answer."
—Author Unknown

TWO DAYS AFTER I GAVE THANKS THAT THE BOYS HADN'T ASKED how two dads have a baby, they asked.

We were on our way to the post office.

"Mom?" inquired Jack. "I was just wondering. Um, so, when two dads have a baby? Like, how does that work?'"

I'd barely inhaled in preparation to deliver an answer to which I hadn't yet given nearly enough thought.

"They poop it out," responded Henry.

"Um, that's not altogether true," I corrected. "Let's discuss this after we get out of the post office."

I was already irrelevant to the conversation.

"They don't poop it out, Henry," Jack retorted." Have you ever *seen* a pregnant man?"

"Well," chimed in Grace, "There is that one man who was on *The Today Show*, but I don't think he's really a man and…"

"STOP! This conversation is over. We'll begin it again after we are finished in the post office, and I truly cannot wait," I admonished.

This particular post office is notoriously busy, so I was thrilled to be fourth in line. My euphoria, however, was quickly decimated by the site of my worst nightmare donning the entrance.

No, it was not Mitchell, Cam, and Lily from *Modern Family*. It was a gentleman who likely only needed to mail a birthday card to his mother. To be clear, *that* isn't my worst nightmare…on a Saturday…when I am permitted a solo outing to the post office. But on a Monday, as a mother (specifically, as a mother of Two, Three, and Four), he was my worst nightmare.

He had no idea what he'd walked into. It was as though the world went into slow motion as I watched Three's mouth slowly open—and my hand reach up in an attempt to cover it.

I wasn't fast enough.

The whole post office was suddenly and irreparably privy to Henry's latest observation.

"Mom, that guy's not wearing a SHIRT!"

"Nope, he's not!" I confirmed, trying to sound perky and accepting. "I think he rode his bike here!"

"Yeah, he's all SWEATY!" proclaimed Four, completely disgusted.

Mm-hm.

"And he has a LOT of kakoos," further reported Four.

"Tattoos," corrected Two (loudly), "With Ts, not Ks."

By this point, the shirtless, sweaty, tattoo-covered patron was, thankfully, not glaring at us or flashing the gang sign for "I'll get you outside."

Instead, he was trying to hide his laughter. Perhaps this wasn't his first encounter with expressive children?

"Um, isn't it illegal to be in here without a shirt on?" asked Two.

"Next!" called John, my favorite postal clerk.

Thank God.

As we stood at the counter for what felt like 124 minutes, all five children stared at the spectacle of the hour while I continued nervously multi-tasking.

"Turn around! First class, please. Now! No, no, John, not you. Henry, stop whispering! Yes, one book of stamps, please. George, I don't KNOW why he has an eagle kakood on his chest. That's all John; have a great day."

"I like it!" declared Henry out of nowhere.

"You like what, Henry?" (No, I don't know what possessed me to ask.)

"That eagle on his chest," still staring, and now demonstratively pointing at the man who will now forever be known by my children as Eagle Man.

Great.

On our way out, the kids nearly tripped over one another as they refused to transfer their gaze from Eagle Man's chest. Four and I simultaneously noticed what I knew was the nail in the coffin.

Amazingly, Four said nothing. He simply opened his eyes as wide as anatomically possible, looked away from Eagle Man, glued his arms to his sides, and walked as quickly as his life-altering state of shock would allow him.

And then I felt tugging on my arm.

"Mom, why does he have rings in his…you know…?" asked Henry, discreetly pointing at his own chest.

The good news was that the kids were so enthralled with talking about Eagle Man for the next few hours that they completely forgot their question about how two dads have a baby.

After watching a few episodes, David and I decided that *Modern Family* is okay for the kids to watch with us on occasion, and they got to see firsthand how Cam and Mitchell adopted Lily. They thought it was lovely. To them, it's just one more way families are created. George is even on the lookout for a Diana Ross wig for

Nina just like the one Cam put on Lily.

The conversations we think are going to be the hardest often turn out to be not that bad at all. Another example is the time I had to have "the talk" with Grace, and upon its conclusion, she looked pensively toward the ceiling while I prepared to admit, "Yes, Papa and I did do that four times." Instead, she asked if I could find some pictures of a uterus for her to examine. She was curious about where in a woman's body the uterus resides. Also, what sperm look like. And that was that.

Then there was the day that Jack asked me where dirt comes from. Now that *really* threw me for a loop.

Rule 20
Have No Expectations (but Expect the Unexpected)

"A characteristic of the normal child is
he doesn't act that way very often."
—Author Unknown

I LOVE GAYLE KING. I USED TO LISTEN TO HER DAILY ON XM satellite radio. Until I got Sirius, which came with dear Lulu. Which was great because I love "Homegrown" with Andrew Beckman and Tony Bielaczyc on the Martha Stewart channel, as well as Doctor Radio, which fairly effectively convinces me by lunchtime that I have at least four maladies (it's channel 114 should you wish to join me in hypochondrial bliss).

But I missed the Oprah channel. That is, until someone mentioned that I could pay an extra four dollars per month and get some of the "cross-over" channels—including Oprah. Which I instructed David to do. Immediately. Because when summer hits, moms had better have a plan for surviving car rides during which someone's finger is always thinking about possibly maybe touching someone else's shoelace, which is, obviously, a perfectly valid reason for World War 3 to commence.

Summer comes upon mothers suddenly and violently. On Day

1 of summer vacation, I know that there are 68 days left. Not that I'm counting. Last summer, by 2:12 p.m. on that first fateful day, I'd already learned seven valuable ways that having no expectations can help one maintain Summer Break Sanity. I understand that even more tips are dispensed through the local community college's one-credit course titled, can you believe it, "Summer Break Sanity 101." Sadly, however, it's offered only at noon on Wednesdays.

1. Taking five kids grocery shopping when it's already 97 degrees out at 9:00 a.m.? Two words: Don't. Okay, that's one word, but it's the contraction of Do Not, which *is* two words. I'll blame my poor math skills on exhaustion, as I *just* took five kids grocery shopping, and it's already 97 degrees at 9:00 a.m.

2. If you choose to take five kids grocery shopping when it's already 97 degrees at 9:00 a.m., and you ask a kid to go get two canteloupes, and he appears in front of you with them stuffed up his shirt while his brothers crack up until tears stream down their faces, don't be surprised. And, an additional piece of advice from Big Daddy: don't be miffed either. After all, "You're the one who asked me to get two canteloupes!" Touche.

3. When you take the kids to the bookstore so that they can each pick out a summer reading book, anticipate staying thirty minutes longer than planned in order to engage in not-so-peaceful negotiations over your steadfast belief that *Captain Underpants Down Under, SpongeBob Takes Tahiti*, and anything that plays music and comes with a designated age range of 2-4 doesn't qualify. If you're smart enough to declare these rules before you enter the store, be forewarned that even if—at the moment you deliver the message—the kids are quiet as mice and looking right at you, they are not listening.

4. Seven-year-olds will enter into loud debate with other 7-year-olds (and a 4-year-old) in the bookstore over whether or not they need to be wearing deodorant.

5. Almost-10-year-olds will retort (loudly) that babies don't need to wear deodorant, after which the debate will turn briskly and tragically to the topic of who in the family is the biggest baby.

6. Bookstore train tables erected with the under-3 set in mind appeal most to the over-7 set. When you hear one of your kids holler, "The green caboose is *mine*, smelly underwear head!" it's truly in your best interest to pretend you entered the store solo.

7. A Starbucks iced, grande, soy, green tea latte is the perfect reward for enduring an "eventful" morning. Seriously, try it. It's the prettiest drink I've ever ordered and one of my staple treats. Also on the list, a white chocolate raspberry iced coffee with just a smidge of half and half. Sierra the Barista made it one morning before the rush hit the drive-thru, and she let me sample it. It rocked my world. I think Starbucks needs to officially put it on the menu and name it The Sierra.

Low expectations: they aren't pessimistic; they're realistic. And they leave you with nowhere to go but up.

When moms ask me for tips on flying with young children, I give them some of my more tangible tried-and-true standbys, but also tell them that the smartest things to pack in their carry-on are a sense of humor and low expectations. Just expect the worst. It can't get worse than the worst, right? I've known many a woman who adopted this approach and was pleasantly surprised after the flight, noting, "Well, Charlie threw up ten minutes in, Oliver smacked the flight attendant across the face, and Lily said "boob" over and over again for a hour. It wasn't so bad!"

Rule 21
Know What Inspires You

———————— ·❖· ————————

"What would you attempt, if you knew you could not fail?"
—Author Unknown

I HATE RUNNING. I'VE MENTIONED THAT, RIGHT? SO OUT OF necessity I have a secret source of inspiration for getting through a run when I'm hating every step—or getting through any other experience, for that matter, when I need anything from a little help to downright divine intervention.

Have you seen the video that circulates on YouTube called, "Where the Hell is Matt? (2008)" wherein Matt Harding and his unique dance make their way around the world?

If you haven't seen it, and you have Internet access, go and watch it. Go to YouTube.com and type "Where the Hell is Matt" in the search field. Even if you *have* seen it, watch it again. It's just that great.

There is no fancy degree behind what he's done. There's no special training. If you watch interviews with him, he hasn't even yet decided what he wants to be when he grows up.

But here he is, dancing in a demilitarized zone in Korea (where you know the guard in the background wants to say, "What the hell?" so badly). Dancing with kids in Madagascar and Zambia and Timbuktu and Soweto, South Africa—kids who lack a great deal materially, including shoes, but appear happier than many kids wandering around the USA in their $100 sneakers, texting on iPhones, and drinking $6 venti Frappaccinos.

Dancing amidst hundreds of perfectly red crabs on, appropriately enough, Christmas Island. Dancing in the rain—not in his front yard but in Zanzibar. He doesn't just stop to smell the flowers, he dances among them in The Netherlands.

He dances with a woman in a red shirt in Brisbane, Australia who has joy emanating from her pores, and with the natives in Papua New Guinea who, truthfully, scare me a little but with whom I'd totally love to have dinner. Dancing next to a camel in Jordan who is—if you look closely enough—I think, smiling. Practically washed to sea by a wave while dancing in Tongatapu, Tonga.

My favorite part is the clip of Auki, Solomon Islands, when Matt stops dancing and slightly covers his mouth, appearing to giggle. It's as though he's in absolute awe of the happiness that surrounds him, and of what he's done (or maybe he's just utterly exhausted).

Look closely at the people in this video. Notice the joy on all their faces. They're doing nothing but dancing. That's it. They're not working. They're not buying something. They're not being applauded or validated by anyone on the outside. They're just dancing. This is how desperate people are just to be happy. For no reason at all.

The very idea that this Matt traveled to all of these places and got all of these people to dance, to just dance, and in those moments, to forget all their other worries, is enough inspiration for me any day.

It reminds me of possibilities. Of all that we can do—if only we believe. Matt is my favorite kind of person. He's a Why Not? guy. And when you approach everything you do with that attitude, everything is possible.

I know; Matt doesn't have kids. He doesn't have a family to worry about. He doesn't have the same responsibilities you or I might claim keep us from dancing. But you can bet that many of the people who got up and danced with him do.

When I feel like I can't run a mile, or run a company, or run a household while my hair is glowing, or run after one more kid who's broken loose and is darting toward the down escalator, I think of this video, or I watch it, or I play "Praan," the soundtrack they're dancing to, which I downloaded from iTunes. It changes everything.

Go and watch the video again. Believe in the moment when you get goosebumps and feel invincible. If Matt can dance in the demilitarized zone of Korea, you, my friend, can do anything you want.

It doesn't stop with Matt, however. A 4-year-old who can play the drums about as well as Travis Barker? (I simultaneously applaud and pity his parents for supporting his hobby!); or the random outburst of hundreds of people singing and dancing to "Do-Re-Mi" from *The Sound of Music* in Belgium's Central Station—reportedly carried out with no formal rehearsal beforehand? Each time I watch it I can't help but smile—more at the unsuspecting passengers' reactions than the performance itself! And how about Susan Boyle's audition for *Britain's Got Talent?* The look in Simon Cowell's eyes says it all.

When something inspires you, consider the reasons why. Is it the music? Is it the actions? Is it an I-have-to-get-off-this-couch-right-now burst of inspiration to research something, learn about something, or practice something? Learning why something touches your heart can provide great insight into an activity that perhaps you'd enjoy getting involved with one some level.

After I heard Susan Boyle sing "Wild Horses" on *America's Got Talent*, I vowed to buy her CD the moment it was released. I don't even really like the song all that much. But her voice reminds me of all that is possible. It reminds me that the crowd that at first looks at someone with skepticism is perhaps in for the biggest shock of its life. Another CD that I'll be purchasing the day it's released? Barbara Padilla's. Also from *America's Got Talent*, but seriously, *how* was she not discovered prior to this show? When I watch her sing, "Ave Maria," I come close to losing my mind to a tidal wave of awe.

I've realized that what inspires me most often is music. Whether it's a previously undiscovered talent or a piece that stirs emotion, the right music can, for me, bring about everything from a mad cleaning frenzy to a piece of writing that seems to come from out of nowhere. Focusing on my love of music helped me to realize how much I'd like to learn to play the guitar. So I bought one for myself last year for Christmas. I'd also like to again take up the piano, and I hope to add a baby grand to the house in the next few years.

When you identify that consistent source of personal inspiration, you'll know it because you'll feel a joy and a motivation somewhere deep inside—a place you didn't even know existed.

I believe, by the way, that this feeling is so great because it's not a human feeling at all. It's your spirit rejoicing at being discovered and paid attention.

There is a whole slew of inspiring stories and videos available to jumpstart your discovery of what elicits this feeling in you. If you go to this book's page on my website (elizabethlyons.com) you can check out the Inspiration section for links to those I've most enjoyed. I add to them regularly. Begin building your own list and refer to it often. The more frequently you connect with your spirit in this way, the more accessible it will be to you on a daily basis.

Rule 22
Switch Hats with Grace and Humility

—∞—

"If you can't ride two horses at once,
you shouldn't be in the circus."
—American Proverb

A N EXCERPT FROM THE NOTEBOOKS OF LAZARUS LONG FROM Robert Heinlein's *Time Enough for Love* reads, "A human being should be able to change a diaper, plan an invasion, butcher a hog, conn a ship, design a building, write a sonnet, balance accounts, build a wall, set a bone, comfort the dying, take orders, give orders, cooperate, act alone, solve equations, analyze a new problem, pitch manure, program a computer, cook a tasty meal, fight efficiently..."

These notebooks were surely written in the 1800s. Had they been written in the last quarter century, the excerpt would obviously begin with "A *mom* should be able to..." and end with "before noon."

It occurs to me that, perhaps, I should not tell you what I'm about to. So please know that I did consider that option. But in the interest of full disclosure, I feel it's essential to...well...disclose.

I've touted the many positive qualities of Humphrey, our 2-year-old chocolate merle (untrained) Cockapoo, whom I love tremendously—if for no other reason than that he loves me unconditionally. Like, when I take him to Petco, he doesn't use phrases like "worst ever" and "totally wrong" if I refuse to buy him a lollipop in the checkout line.

One evening, however, he did not do himself any favors in terms of my (or anyone else's) love for him.

Let me begin with a bit of important background information. When Humphrey disappears underneath our bed, it's for one reason and one reason only: he's eating something he shouldn't be eating. Like a diaper, or a bag of lollipops, or my underwear.

So when I spied him stealthily slithering underneath our bed much like Catherine Zeta Jones dipped underneath laser alarm triggers in *Entrapment*, I knew something was up.

"Out!" I called.

And out he came. (See what I mean? Someone listening—and responding—after only one request. It's unheard of. And appreciated.)

I peeked under the bed to retrieve what I was confident was nothing more than the bedtime diaper I'd inadvertently left on the floor of the baby's room.

What I found instead was—understandably I'm sure—not surprising, yet most unacceptable.

Poop.

How, I wondered, *did this dog crawl under here and poop?*

Now, at the very moment I yelled, "Out!" Humphrey was retrieving a wipe from under the bed, leading me to believe—understandably, I'm sure—that the wipe had come from the aforementioned diaper (as had, one would assume, the poop).

I reached in with the wipe Humphrey so generously provided and pulled out the poop. At which point, I became very concerned. The poop had blood all over it.

I know this is getting more disgusting with each passing line. But hang on. You've gotten this far. It would be a shame to miss the punch line now.

"Oh, my poor Humphrey!" I exclaimed with great despair. "Something is very, very wrong. What has happened to you? David! I need the number to the vet…*right now!*"

It was then, in that moment of total panic and utter desperation that I realized that the blood-covered piece of poop I was holding in my hand was more than a piece of poop.

For it had a head.

And whiskers.

Did you gag yet?

Yes, the Humpster had found what I can only hope was an already dead mouse and brought it in for a midnight snack under my bed.

But it gets worse.

Of course, I nearly lost my mind. I squealed at much the same decibel that, I'm sure, Stuart Little did when he met his maker. David sauntered in and after learning what had happened, ordered me to put the dog in his kennel.

Which I did.

When I turned around to ask for help in removing this poor, poor creature from our home, David was no longer there. And where was he? Oh, yes, on the countertop. He's 6-foot-7, folks, and he was on the countertop. Completely unwilling to help, and distraught that his entire evening was ruined because he could no longer swallow the ice cream sundae he'd just prepared for himself.

In what can only be described as sorrowful acceptance of the situation, I went outside, grabbed a shovel, disposed of Mr. Little, thoroughly canvassed every square inch of space under our bed to be sure there were no legs, intestines, or, God help me, tail remaining, and proceeded (in response to what I'd characterize as the most politely uttered do-it-now-or-I'm-outta-here request in the history of wedded bliss) to strip the bed and launder it all on the sanitary cycle. Just in case the dog had breathed on our sheets after he munched on his dessert.

I then made myself a sundae. With fudge. And chocolate chips. There you have it. Mom by day; animal control officer by night.

One morning after I asked the kids to go upstairs and brush their teeth before school, Grace informed me that she could do no such thing.

"Why not?"

"Because my sink is full of water, and it won't drain."

"Did you tell your father about this?"

"Yeah. He said you'd fix it."

Of course he did.

That day after school, I asked Grace to follow me upstairs so that I could show her how to remedy a clogged sink.

"Seriously?" asked Grace. "That sounds disgusting. You're not going to make me *do* it, are you?"

"Depends on whether or not you change your tone."

Upstairs we went. I put a bucket underneath the sink, wedged myself inside the cabinet and explained that you unscrew the P-trap from the other pipes and carefully remove it, allowing the water and, hopefully, whatever's clogging the sink to drop into the bucket.

"Okay, do you see this Grace?" I asked, anxious to showcase exactly what had caused the situation to begin with.

"Grace?"

"GRACE!"

"WHAT!" Grace answered from the loft.

"Grace, what are you doing? Where *are* you? You're supposed to be paying attention!"

"Well, I didn't know. You're all stuck up in the cabinet and stuff. I couldn't see anyway."

I took a few moments to calmly explain that hair that's been brushed off the heads of her American Girl dolls needs to be put in the trash, not down the drain.

By this point, Jack had arrived on the scene.

"Mom, you know I'll help you with a lot of things, but *this* is *disgusting!*"

Mm-hm.

"Jack, there's one thing I think that your future wife would appreciate my mentioning right now."

"Yes?" he asked, riveted.

"In most households—not all, but most—the dad is the one who remedies plumbing disasters. Just so you know."

"Can you hire someone to do it?" he asked.

"You can. But it costs more than it needs to. It's not that hard to do yourself."

"You mean, like tile?"

"Right."

You see, when we moved into our house, I wanted the entire front porch to be tiled with six-inch by six-inch slate tiles.

How hard can it be? I wondered. After all, I'd tiled before.

Let's just say that I don't recommend tiles smaller than twenty-by-twenty when doing an area larger than four feet by four feet, and I don't recommend a natural stone under any circumstances if you're doing the job yourself.

That tiling project took three weeks, included many late nights, and required an entire day with a whole jar of Eucerin lotion spread onto my hands—which were then encased in silk gloves.

It's no secret that moms wear many hats. This is where estimates of how much moms should be paid based on the many jobs they do come from. I've learned that wearing many hats is simply part of our "job." We've been screaming it from the rooftops for decades and we'll likely still be screaming it from the rooftops decades from now if December 21, 2012 doesn't bring all the insanity to a halt in a hurry.

I ask David constantly, "Aren't you glad your wife fixes toilets?" and "Aren't you glad your wife can bargain shop like nobody's business?" And then, when there's a rattlesnake in the garden, David says, "Aren't you glad your husband isn't afraid of rattlesnakes?" (Stay tuned for the backstory on this one).

Rule 23
There's Nothing Wrong with a Little Bribery

---···◁∞▷···---

*"The thing that impresses me most about
America is the way parents obey their children."*
—Edward, Duke of Windsor

TODAY WAS GEORGE'S FIRST DAY OF KINDERGARTEN. HE ONLY had a half session, meaning that he was there just long enough to prevent me from doing any major damage in JoAnn's, Target, or Bed Bath & Beyond.

This is George's third year at the same school. It's a Montessori school, so the classes are a mixture of kids from age three to age six. Nothing is different this year versus last year. He has the same teachers, many of the same classmates, and the same classroom.

Still, he was a bit hesitant.

"George, you're big man on campus this year—a kindergartner!" I encouraged. "I can't wait to hear all about your day!" I continued, gently nudging him into the classroom.

"I don't want to go," he declared.

"George, it's a short class today." (No, I wasn't sure what I'd do the following week when the full three-hour day kicked in. I figured I'd worry about it on Monday.)

Finally, after seven or eight minutes of stalling, George moved his left foot...then his right foot...then his left foot...forward an inch at a time until he was almost over the threshold. At which point, one of his teachers approached.

"George, we're so glad to see you! We're so happy to have you coming into the classroom!"

"I'm only coming in because Mom said that if I did, she'd get me anything I wanted."

It's true.

Look, you gotta do what you gotta do. And today, what I had to do was purchase gum in a blue package, chocolate milk with whip and chocolate drizzle but no ice, and a strawberry muffin. Starbucks doesn't yet make a strawberry muffin, so after I explained to Craig the Barista that I was holding him and him alone personally accountable for the tantrum that would likely ensue 90 minutes later (he officially accepted all responsibility), I went with an old-fashioned chocolate donut. Chocolate donuts never fail. Right?

I never thought I'd give terribly much thought to the minute details of our kids' education. I think I simply assumed, *How hard can it be? Move into a good school district, hope no one ever gets (or gives) a swirl or a Texas wedgie, and pray they learn enough to be able to read road signs and add currency by the time they're 40.*

You know what they say about assuming.

In a nutshell, I've found myself looking critically at each grade's curriculum. Which I am totally qualified to do. After all, I have a degree in Japanese.

Next year, our oldest makes the leap to middle school. Which means that the elementary school rebels who say "hell" will be replaced by middle school rebels who tell others to go there as they make their way to the basketball courts for a pre-algebra smoke or drag off an unsuspecting sixth-grader to the bathroom for a pre-calculus swirl.

I know, kids have to learn how to navigate the world and the 10-year-old smokers (and swirl givers) who inhabit it, but I'm just saying, when it's your kid, you want to put them into a bubble where everyone says "ma'am" and "please" and the word "fart" was never invented.

I've begun exploring charter schools for Grace to attend during her formative middle school years. She's not pleased.

"Will they have lockers at a charter middle school?" she asked.

This is a huge and understandable concern for a 10-year-old girl. Because a proper middle school must come equipped with three things: a locker (for storage of Zac Efron pictures), a friend with a cell phone that texts, and a class or two in parental bribery.

After 34 minutes, I came close to convincing Boo that a locker (or the lack thereof) isn't the be-all-end-all of middle school. I informed her that there are potentially more exciting things to look forward to.

She became curious.

"What kinds of exciting things?" she asked.

"Well," I responded, seeing the window of opportunity opening, "One of the schools I'm looking at has drama, art, and a guitar club. And they even start teaching Latin in sixth grade."

She visibly perked up. I think I even saw the formation of a few goosebumps.

"You mean, like, pig Latin?" she inquired.

"Um, no. Like real Latin."

"Oh," she said, deflated. "Well, if they had pig Latin, you could send me there for sure. But regular Latin? I don't know."

Bribery. Sometimes it's served with breakfast. Other times, as a carefully disguised side order with dinner. On occasion, it's front and center on the All-Day Dining menu. In that spirit, I'm thinking I'm going to do whatever I must to ensure that the school of my choice has lockers. And I will personally provide Grace an up-to-date photograph of Zac Efron to hang inside it.

And I'm okay with that approach. Because I've learned to be at peace with the parenting strategies I choose on any given day. I don't utilize illegal tactics, and if I have to bribe a child or a spouse or a dog here or there, so be it.

You've got to be able to channel Stuart Smalley from *Saturday Night Live* as you look into the mirror and say, "I'm smart enough, I'm good enough, I'm cute enough, and even if the other parents think I'm an idiot, I'm okay with it. Because gosh darn it, it's the only way I'll make it through this day."

There, you feel better already, don't you.

Rule 24
Repeat After Me: I'm a Good Mom
(Even if I Don't Scrapbook)

"Memories, like the corners of my mind."
—Barbra Streisand

I READ A QUOTE THE OTHER DAY: "A DAY WITHOUT SCRAPBOOKING is a day without sunshine." If that's the case, I'm screwed.

A great benefit of blogging is that, if you type quickly, you can fairly well document the hysteria of your children's younger years in a short timeframe. I knew something like this would come along eventually. And I fervently prayed for it when a few of my friends were creating scrapbook pages that literally rose from their binding. 3-D castles anyone?

No.

I simply don't scrapbook. I don't like it. There, I said it. I'm an anti-scrapbook-ite.

When our kids were younger and said or did something funny (or ridiculous) enough that I orally regaled someone with it, that someone inevitably advised, "You'd better write that down!"

This concerned me. I hadn't time to find a pen let alone write anything down.

Will I really forget all of this? I wondered. *Will I only remember the moments that involved unpleasantries?*

My solution was found in Tupperware (isn't it always?). A little see-through box with a hinged lid served as the temporary burial grounds for humorous sayings and unforgettable choices that would, after a week's time, become not only forgettable but forgotten.

The idea was that I'd jot down the basics of a phrase or incident onto a scrap of paper, toss it into the Tupperware box, and return to the box at a later date to document them more formally. I had no idea what that meant (and still don't), but in just a few seconds, I could release one memory from my brain onto a piece of paper and forget it. At least until I found time and a non-scrapbooking approach to doing something nicer with it.

I found one of my boxes the other day—I have a few—and began to go through it. It was like unearthing a time capsule. I'm so glad for the Tupperware Treasure Box, for without it, I would never have remembered the day that I was going through alphabet flash cards with Jack and Henry (otherwise known as Two and Three), who were probably pushing four years of age and still thought "Q" was a number.

I held up the letter "A."

"Guys, what letter is this?" I asked with the hope and faith of Noah.

"I don't know," responded Jack.

I held up the letter "F."

"Guys, what letter is this?" I asked.

"I don't know," responded Jack.

"Okay, let's try this differently. What letter sounds like fffff?"

"Oh, I know!" responded Jack, his hand shooting into the air. "Fee!"

I tried to contain my frustration. "Um, that's not a letter,"

I explained.

"Give me one," requested Henry.

I held up the letter I. "What's this letter?" I asked.

"I don't know," responded Henry.

"I'll give you a hint," I offered. "It's the first letter in the word iiiice Cream."

"Oh, I know!" sang Henry, bouncing in on the couch *and* stretching his hand toward the ceiling.

"Cone!"

I vaguely remember crying myself to sleep that evening, sure that those two would never be able to read a road sign, would therefore never pass their driving test, and would (therefore) never be able to move out. Not that I'm looking forward to that day. Because I'm not. But in my overall life plan, it does happen. At some point. Just sayin'.

I'm pleased to report that they do finally know the alphabet. However the other day Henry asked me what kind of seeds you need to plant to grow Cajun spiced turkey breast.

We all want to keep track of the milestones, the comments you couldn't have made up if you tried, and the photos that prove we tried to make a Dora the Explorer cake for our daughter's third birthday.

I'm a fan of an online scrapbooking service called How Fast They Grow. They tout themselves as the "Home of the 7-minute scrapbook page." That's my kind of scrapbooking!

Another solution to documenting out-and-about-moments-worth-remembering is a small notebook I keep in my purse (*with* a pen—because it's the one thing I never seem to have when I need it).

I've also been known to utilize the memo pad on my Black-Berry (after Grace showed me where to find it and how to use it) to quickly type out the basics of a comment made in the car—

when I "wasn't listening,"—the premise for a new blog post, or the precise time and location of Henry's first correct pronunciation of "breakfast."

Rule 25
Be the Teacher Only 97% of the Time

"While we try to teach our children all about life,
our children teach us what life is all about."
—Angela Schwindt

ONE DAY GRACE BURST IN THE BACK DOOR, A LOOK OF SHEER terror covering her otherwise innocent face.

"MOTHER!" she shouted. "YOUR RED PEPPER IS FINAL-LY RED!"

"That's awesome, Gracey, thank you!" I responded. This was, in fact, most exciting news, as my organic garden is much slower to deliver sustenance than its overly fertilized counterparts.

"But does this find really require yelling?"

"Yes, yes it does!" continued Grace. "You see, I went to pick it for you, and as I reached my hand in, I saw a HEAD!"

She had my attention.

"What kind of a head?" I asked, quite sure that I did not want an answer.

"Um, that of a SNAKE! WITH NO EYES!"

The fact that she stayed around long enough to ascertain wheth-er or not the snake had eyes was a clear indication that, while

Grace and I apparently look exactly alike, the genes that fostered the miraculous creation of her brain did not come from me.

Long story short, there was a snake in my garden. A rattle-snake. A baby rattlesnake. Which was dead. Because it had gotten trapped in the netting that I'd put over my peppers. To keep out birds and rabbits. Not snakes.

At that moment, I sadly declared my gardening days over, told everyone to stay inside, and called David to let him know there was a really cool, headless nightmare in the garden that required his prompt attention.

Fast-forward a week.

As I threw a final handful of chopped vegetables into the soup pot, I thought aloud, "This soup needs something."

"How about some thyme?" suggested Grace, snake whisperer and aspiring chef.

"Nope," I responded. "Not going into the garden. Not gonna do it."

And then, without so much as blinking, she said, "Leave the past behind you, Mom. Leave the past behind you."

Kind of hard to argue with that—on so many levels. So with my proverbial tail between my legs, out I went to the garden. In 118 degrees. Wearing knee-high boots and carrying a shovel.

David occasionally goes hunting in Sedona, and takes Grace with him. He drops her off at her cousin's to spend the night. Both she and her cousin get so excited that neither of them sleeps, which makes our life super fun for the next 48 hours while she recovers.

Grace and I have our girly days when we go shopping, out to eat, whatever. We've also gone on several trips together.

I spent the vast majority of Henry's life with him from the age of four months until he turned three. As the second-born twin—and one who took his sweet time entering this world, waiting until the obstetrician was holding surgical tools in hand and instructing the anesthesiologist to kick the epidural up 14 notches—he endured a rather traumatic birth, and as a result, received a good bit of therapy outside the house. I was required to do so much therapy homework with him *inside* the house that we were pretty tightly connected to one another, literally and figuratively, for many years.

Not surprisingly, in hindsight, Jack (even at only 18 months of age) often acted in the capacity of the therapist's assistant, doing things we never would have thought of in order to encourage Henry to speak or move. The kid could totally fend for himself, while Henry wouldn't touch food or move a limb to get anything he wanted. Trust me, I profusely thanked God for Jack's self-sufficient nature each time I got off my rear end to grab Henry a rattle. Or a Cheerio.

Then there's George. George didn't cut the cord until he was three-and-a-half. As I've mentioned, for the first 1,277 or so days of his life, he was the heaviest fashion accessory I'd ever worn. And then one day, he instructed me to "talk to the hand," wanting nothing more to do with me.

Which was somewhat jarring.

He became Daddy's Boy in the blink of an eye and, as I mentioned earlier, dedicated all holiday wishes— including those reserved for the woman who nurtured him in utero for forty-and-a-half weeks—exclusively to his father.

So Jack sort of got the shaft, as they say. And I've greatly enjoying making it up to him.

The kid is quite multi-faceted, much like his father. He's athletic and domestic and kind and funny. And while he won't help me remove doll hair from a drain pipe, he's happy to haul bag after bag of organic compost from Lulu's trunk to the garden, which is greatly appreciated because, let's be honest, the stuff stinks.

One afternoon I asked him to go with me on a mountain bike ride into—can you guess—the mountains. Our neighbors told us about a trail behind our house that sounded fun.

Of course, he agreed.

On the way up the hill (the very steep hill), I heard him from behind profess, "I love my life."

Seven-year-old boys love a lot of things: their toys, Wii, days off from school, ice cream, hitting their sister, and breaking things, for starters.

But to say, "I love my *life*" as a 7-year-old?

I somehow doubt that happens all that often.

It was the most Zen statement he's ever made—totally void of materialism and focused only on how beautiful the day was, the fact that he was out enjoying it on his bike and, I like to think, the fact that we were out and about together.

We headed toward the trail.

Now, let me preface what's coming by revealing that I was not wearing a helmet. But I survived. Barely. And I wrote "Liz Helmet" on the Target list the minute we returned home.

When you're mountain biking with your 7-year-old (and looking *muy* cool with the baby seat on the back of your most fabulous Diamondback mountain bike—the one given to you by your most fabulous husband 11 years ago though not ridden until…well… that very day because you got pregnant about six minutes after the gift was presented and stayed that way until…well…recently), and every eight minutes or so that 7-year-old turns his head 180-degrees to inquire, "Mom? You okay back there?" you start to feel a bit…well…old.

We came upon a long, steep downhill. It was paved with nothing but gravel, and in case I forgot to mention it, I wasn't wearing a helmet.

I told Jack, as we sat perched atop this very steep hill aware that there was nowhere to go *but* down, that this is why we wear helmets. So that if you go over the handlebars and hit your head on a rock, the helmet protects your very delicate and important brain.

The entire way down I chanted, "Do not go over the handlebars. Do not go over the handlebars."

We made it to the bottom, and Jack declared, "Mom, if we hit another hill like that, I'm going first. I think I need to test it for you. And do you have a *clue* where this path will end up?"

No sir. I do not.

So, another hill we hit and, as promised, Jack raised his hand and said, "Stop! I'm going first."

I truly felt younger than seven.

After we made it down that hill (with the damn baby seat bouncing like mad the whole way down), Jack said, "Mom, you really do need a helmet. Because if you fall and get hurt, I'll be lost."

"Jack, somehow I am quite confident that you would find your way home."

"Well, that's true," he confided. "But I wouldn't know what to do with your body."

Huh?

"Jack, this raises an excellent point. Next time we do this, I'm bringing (along with a helmet) my cell phone."

"Yeah, you need to teach me how to use that. In case I have to get someone to come get your body."

Seriously?

An hour later we (finally) arrived at an outlet from which I thought we could get home. As we came up and over the hill, we saw David, Nina, and George.

"Good God, where did you come from?" asked David.

"Don't ask," responded Jack.

I was exhausted. But as we rode down the sidewalk, I looked up and boldly stated, "I love my life."

We focus a lot as parents on the fact that we're expected to teach our kids. And we are. But we can't lose sight of what we can learn from them.

When suffering from a severe case of writer's block, I often ask my kids to think of something I should write about. This works brilliantly when I'm working on one of my children's books because who better to think of something kids would find funny than kids?

Sometimes, the answers to our problems are much more simple than we make them. Case in point, one day when we were still living in Chicago, and the kids wanted to go outside, I said it was too cold. Grace, a mere 4-year-old at the time, replied, "So put on a coat."

Sometimes, it's just that simple!

Rule 26
Pick Battles Wisely

"Pick battles big enough to matter,
not small enough to win."
—Jonathan Kozol

HERE'S THE CONVERSATION THAT ENSUED ONE MORNING EN route to school.

"You know what, Mom?" asked Henry.

"What?"

"Some of the girls in my class? Well, they think I'm hot."

I tried to remain calm.

"Henry, what does that mean exactly?"

"It means that they think I'm cute and handsome and they want to be my girlfriend."

"And," contributed Jack, "when a girl is hot, it means she's pretty and gorgeous."

"Uh-huh. Can we just say people are pretty or cute? Can we not use the word 'hot'?"

"No," responded Henry. "I'm hot. That's what they said."

"Uh-huh. Henry, do you have a girlfriend? Because the last time I asked you said 'Absolutely not!'"

"Yeah, I have a few."

"A few?" I asked, a bit concerned. "I really think it's polite to have only one at a time."

"Okay," agreed Henry. "Well then I pick Tiffany."

"Why Tiffany?"

"Because she has big front teeth like I do."

"Uh-huh. Well, it's important to choose someone with whom you have something in common."

"Well," piped in Jack, "I still have six or seven girlfriends. And I'm not going to have just one. I mean, I don't want to hurt anyone's feelings."

I chose not to take the time to explain the fundamentals of dating one person at a time, or to take great issue with referring to oneself or one's peers as "hot." I've learned that if you don't pick your battles, you'll be battling all day every day until the end of time. I'm sure that one day (when they're 16), it won't be acceptable to have seven girlfriends, and I'm sure those seven girls will let Jack know as much.

Another area in which I try to stay removed is the kids' apparent career paths. Henry recently announced a desire to be an author. Five minutes later, he'd changed his mind. But for those five minutes, I was so excited.

He asked, "How do I be an author? I don't know how to spell all the words. Do they give me the words and then I just copy them?"

"Um, no. That's not what you do. That's called plagiarism; you get in big trouble for that."

"Well, being an author is too hard then. I'm going to be a Jedi Knight instead."

A few months ago, Grace finally moved on from wanting to be a professional waitress. We didn't think it would ever happen, as she spent the first nine years of her life fully dedicated to a career ascertaining whether or not a guest would like a side of fries—not that there's anything wrong with that. She now wants to be a vet, which I find humorous since she can't even feed her own dog because his dry food is "gross."

You have to decide what really is worth your concern at any point in time. Like, when Jack and Henry call each other "stupid" every once in a while, I let it go. When George washes his hands while singing "Happy Birthday to you; you smell like poo poo," I cringe and plug my ears. When Grace says she can't wait until she's in high school so she can wear high heels every day, I play along (knowing, or at the very least hoping, that she'll realize before then how uncomfortable they are).

Now, the day I found Jack using leftover wood to construct a poorly designed go-cart in the garage? Or the evening one of the kids mentioned his friend's opinion that his *teacher* is "hot?" Or the night Henry called Jack a "Stupid a-hole?" Those were battles I chose to fight. And win.

Rule 27
Emergencies Come with the Territory

⋯⋅◁∞▷⋅⋯

"There cannot be a stressful crisis next week.
My schedule is already full."
—Henry Kissinger

G RACE TAKES TAE KWON DO TWICE A WEEK. SHE LOVES IT. I didn't think she'd attach to it the way she has, but she's most into it. She's been known to do her routines in Barnes & Noble.

One Saturday night, David and I drove her about 40 minutes north to her Tae Kwon Do teacher's studio or dojo, or whatever it's called, to test for her yellow belt. It was very exciting. We thought the testing would take, oh, 15 minutes.

We loved every second of watching her do her thing (with 40 other Tae Kwon Do-ers ranging in age from 4 to 44), but soon realized that 15 minutes wasn't to be. The lady next to us confirmed that the entire event would take two, if not three, hours.

David's mom was at our house with Jack, Henry, and George. David left his cell phone in his truck assuming all would be fine; he didn't want his phone to ring inside the dojo/studio/whatever.

We told David's mom we'd be home around 8:00, so at 7:40 I suggested that David call her to inform her that 8:00 wasn't to be.

He went outside to place the call. A few minutes later, I glanced out of the window and saw him motioning for me to come outside. *Oh great*, I thought, *Who threw up?*"

Thankfully, no one had thrown up. Even better, Henry had fallen off his bike, and there was a concern that he needed stitches.

I completely trust David's mom. I also know that face wounds bleed—a lot. So I thought it was possible that it was bleeding enough to make it look like stitches were needed when, in fact, it perhaps required only a cold compress and a big Backyardigans BandAid.

Interested in a second opinion, I called Heather who, by the grace of God, lives across the street. She agreed to go right over and take a look.

I dialed our house back a few minutes later to receive Heather's assessment.

"Uh...oh...um...yeah," said Heather, trying to remain completely unexcited in front of Henry. "I think we need an ER. Like, perhaps now."

Meanwhile, board breaking was ensuing in the dojo/studio/whatever.

"David," I said, "Grace has never done this. I don't think the white belts do this board breaking thing."

"Yes, they do," he answered.

"I'm sorry, what? She's going to break a board with some part of her body having never practiced that before?"

At least we had a trip to the ER already on the schedule. If anything went awry, she could just tag along.

Grace indeed broke the board—with her foot—and was not injured. Hallelujah. Then another kid incorrectly kicked the board with the top of his foot. I was quite sure he broke his toes. I told his mom I had an extra seat in Heather's ambulance if he needed it.

The coordination began. David is fantastic, but coordination, especially in the midst of an emergency, isn't always his strongest suit. As proof, he suggested that I take his truck to the ER; he would take Grace to the pizza joint next door after the testing was complete. I could then pick them up after the ER visit.

Um, ER visits don't last twenty minutes.

He then suggested that his mom put the three boys in the car and drive them all the way to the dojo/studio/whatever. His mom, Jack, and George would stay at the dojo/studio/whatever while I took Henry to the ER.

Um, no.

The guy next to David asked, "How are you going to handle *this*?"

"Please," I responded out of turn. "This is nothing."

I briefly spoke to Henry on the phone.

"Henry," I explained, "Heather is going to bring you up here."

With zero emotion, he responded, "Yeah. I fell off my bike. I think I need to go to the hopstital (yes, that's how he says it) for stitches."

Jack then wanted to "chat," specifically about the fact that he felt the need to accompany us to the ER. I thanked him for his generous offer, and declined. He fell into a crying heap. I hung up.

Heather put Henry in her car, and brought him up to the dojo/studio/whatever. She then drove us to the ER while David stayed with Grace, planning to get her dinner at 9:30 and take her home.

Thirty minutes later Heather arrived, and off to the ER we went.

We got to the hospital—excuse me, the hopstital—at which point I was able to examine the wound. I, too, had to feign calm. It was not good. Henry climbed out of the car, and as we were walking in he reported, "Mom, that says 'Emergency'."

"Yes, Henry, it does."

"Why doesn't it say 'Room'?"

Who knows.

We got right in. The doctor came in and I communicated my assessment.

"This can't be glued, can it."

"Uh, no."

I had never seen a cut like this outside *Grey's Anatomy*. It literally looked like he had two mouths. He smacked his chin right on the sweet spot where your chin meets your neck, and the whole thing just split open to within a millimeter of the bone.

They applied numbing medicine, and Henry slept through all nine stitches. Heather stood by a bit teary-eyed saying, "Oh, this sweet boy. I think he's my favorite now." She then almost threw up because I had stupidly said something about MRSA, rendering her suddenly and unforgettably aware that she'd touched a chair in the waiting room—and then put gum into her mouth without sanitizing her hands. She could feel the staph infection pulsing through her veins (plus, the stitching process wasn't the prettiest sight in the world, and she did have a front-row seat—seeing how she was acting as the maternal one while I stood by intensely studying the stitching process and wondering whether or not Mc-Steamy would do it differently).

The triage nurse came by to see how Henry was doing.

"I didn't want to overreact," she said, "but that was a very bad cut."

Ya think?

Especially when raising boys, emergencies come with the territory. My motto is that as long as a kid is screaming, whatever's happened to him can be fixed.

When Grace was a new walker, if she looked even slightly like she might topple, I was already underneath her to break her fall. They say that 98 percent of a child's reaction to an injury is based on your reaction, which is unfortunate because when Grace was young, if she rolled over too hard I was like, "OH MY GOD ARE YOU OKAY?" at which point she'd go from laughing to crying hysterically.

But having raised boys for the last eight years, when our youngest crashes headfirst down a flight of stairs, I surprisingly calmly inquire, "Whoa! Was that fun or what?" If it wasn't, she lets me know.

When staying in a hotel, it's advised that you know where the emergency exits are. I advise knowing where the best emergency *rooms* are. Some might say that extra diapers and Cheerios are must-haves when out and about with kids. For me, it's a Mt. Everest-worthy first-aid pack. I've got all the cell phones' In Case of Emergency speed dials programmed. I've taught the kids how to work the car phone in the event that an item they're throwing around hits me by mistake and knocks me out en route to wherever.

Don't view emergencies as an inconvenience. Accept them as a natural part of raising children, and budget them into your daily or weekly schedule. Especially when you're on vacation.

Rule 28
Everybody Loses It On Occasion

.·◁∞▷·.

"Mothers are all slightly insane."
—J.D. Salinger

I T's TRUE. AND PROVIDED IT's NOT IN THE PRESENCE OF A POLICE officer who has pulled you over, it's perfectly fine.

I'll admit, I lost it recently myself. I got too comfortable with an emergency-free streak. Which makes sense given that it had been a long time since our last ER visit. At least three weeks.

As I was concluding a phone call with my sister, I heard a scream. That part wasn't unusual. What was unusual was the sudden sight of George standing in front of me, still screaming, and looking a lot like Carrie in the final scene of the movie by the same name—but with the blood pouring down only the left side of his face.

As the story went, someone (of the male persuasion) threw a Matchbox car at his head. The rest is, as they say, history.

I held a compress on it for a while, then put a BandAid on it, then said some prayers because it was rush hour and I *really* didn't want to head to the ER with all four kids in tow. But, after an hour, the blood was still coming out from underneath the BandAid, and

George was wandering around saying, "I don't feel well. I need to go to the hopstital."

As a compromise, I drove (everyone) to our favorite pediatric urgent care facility. They can do stitches, and the wait isn't nearly what it is at the ER (plus, you can avoid the adult victims of everything from a gunshot wound to the Bubonic Plague, which is always a bonus).

Unfortunately, while I thought this was just a minor laceration, the urgent care doctor didn't agree.

"It's pretty gaping," he said. "You need to go to the hospital ER. They'll need to stitch it and stitch it well so he doesn't get a bad scar."

Super.

We did as we were told, and by some miracle, the ER took us back to triage right away.

After being asked for the sixth time (by the sixth person) how this all happened, I suppose I was feeling a bit defensive about the fact that one of my children had done this to the other. After all, it's far easier to blame it on the neighbor, the protruding oven handle, or the broken sidewalk. So, when the poor nurse politely inquired about the course of events that brought us to her section of the Emergency Room, I calmly responded.

"ONE OF MY KIDS DID THIS TO HIM. OKAY? THERE ARE MANY OF THEM. AND THEY ARE ALWAYS FIGHTING. AND TATTLING. AND FIGHTING. AND TODAY, APPARENTLY, THEY WERE THROWING THINGS. AND ONE OF THOSE THINGS MADE CONTACT WITH THIS POOR CHILD'S FOREHEAD. AND NO, I WAS NOT WATCHING SOAP OPERAS WHEN IT HAPPENED. I WAS ON THE PHONE. AND IT WAS BUSINESS. SORT OF."

Poor woman. She gave me a "you poor thing" look and said, with great empathy, "Oh, I get it completely. I have two boys.

They are always fighting."

In that moment, I didn't think she did get it completely. I think I told her as much. I informed her that I didn't think she could possibly understand that the other day, one of my kids (who shall remain nameless) threw a rock at his sister's face. I didn't think she understood that there isn't a single toy in my house that is played with as intended. I didn't think she understood that our oldest daughter wants to raise a panda bear in our backyard. But she's a nurse, not a therapist, which is, I'm sure, precisely what she was thinking in that moment.

She noted that she could easily glue his head back together and avoid stitches. Super. She asked him if he could lie down.

"Yup!" he responded. "Sho!" (which was his version of "Sure" at the time).

He didn't make a peep as she cleaned and glued. When she was finished he actually said, "Tank you. Tank you, Mom."

You're so welcome, dear.

As we exited the Emergency Room, I realized that perhaps he took the old advice about always having on clean underwear—just in case you're unexpectedly taken to the hospital—to the extreme. It became clear (since his pants were practically falling off) that he didn't appear to be wearing underwear.

"George," I asked, "are you wearing underwear?"

"No."

"Why not?"

"Because I don't need to, Mommy."

I was too tired even to respond. My only thought was, "Who cares."

Rule 29
Breakdowns Are Normal—And Necessary

—◦∞◦—

*"You're only given a little spark of madness.
You mustn't lose it."*
—Robin Williams

I'LL ADMIT, SOMETIMES I FEEL A BIT LIKE A FRAUD. I WRITE AND talk and talk and write about the importance of finding and maintaining balance as a mom. And yet every once in a while, I realize I've gotten to a place where I'm about as balanced as a rabid dog.

It's a hard call when you're someone who makes a living—and by "a living," I mean enough to treat myself to a once-a-quarter pedicure at Nails 'n Things—by teaching others how to do stuff, and you find yourself in a physician-heal-thyself position: do you admit it?

After eight seconds of thought coupled with four kitchen outbursts and two glasses of spilled milk, I decided that you do. This may be the wrong choice. If so, I'll claim momentary ignorance based on the aforementioned chaos ensuing around me.

Another key point which I often make when speaking to groups of expectant or new moms is that anyone who claims they have it together all the time is someone from whom you want to run…fast. It's simply impossible to have all your stuff together all the time.

Just sayin'.

Some days are more challenging than others. With five kids, two dogs, a fish, and two companies (and by companies, I mean formal entities for which I must file tax returns but from which I haven't yet realized much more than $19.83 per week), there's a lot going on. I won't go into all that's going on because it would bore you. And no mother need waste any of the 13.7 free minutes she has each day by being bored. But suffice to say that in the midst of all the chaos, I sometimes lose focus on what's really important. I sail through my day going from task to task to task, should to should to should (even *I* have a hard time completely eliminating this word from my vocabulary), and it never occurs to me that that is the very reason I feel so ungrounded.

Every once in a while, I have a mini breakdown. The last time it happened, I told David that I was going to lose it if I didn't get a five-hour break from chaos, to which he responded, "Aren't you writing a book on how to manage these sorts of feelings?"

Um, yes and no. My rules enable me to manage the chaos a large percentage of the time. But no one is immune to occasionally being so completely overwhelmed by what's going on around her that she has to, somehow, blow off steam.

For me, it's about knowing I'm heading downhill and doing what needs to be done to right it. Sometimes that's a few hours out with a friend. Sometimes it's a few hours alone in a bookstore. Sometimes, it's nothing more prophetic or involved than time. It's about acknowledging that things are crazy, apologizing in advance for any snapping that may occur as a result, and trying to reprioritize and regain focus in order to get oneself back to a place where her husband doesn't want to send her off to a mental hospital.

What's critical is that women know when they're spinning, and know how to identify what will pull them up out of their temporary hell. When they constantly blame their current state on other people or other situations, they're not taking any responsibility. And they are, therefore, relying on other people or other things to make them better. That doesn't always work out real well. Especially when those other people have no idea what they need (are you, too, seeing hints of Rule 16 here?). All of my rules are interconnected. When you get yours in place, you'll likely see how they cross and overlap here and there as well. One is designed to keep the next one in line!

Rule 30
Remember What's Really Important

"Enjoy the little things, for one day you may
look back and realize they were the big things."
—Robert Brault

IN THE MIDST OF RUSHING FROM TASK TO TASK (TO TASK) ONE DAY, in the midst of one of my occasional breakdowns, I realized I needed to do something for Father's Day. The kids usually create memorable and personalized Mother's Day gifts at school, but since Father's Day falls in June, the responsibility for ensuring that the kids acknowledge this momentous celebration falls on me.

I printed out four pieces of paper, each with a set of questions about David for the kids to answer. You know, "I love to do [fill in the blank] with Papa," and so forth.

The third question was, "The thing I love most about Papa is [fill in the blank]."

When I created this, I assumed they'd each fill in the blank with something somewhat "material." Like, "He buys me donuts," or "He takes me golfing," or "He lets us listen to Snoop Dog in the car."

Some of them did that, and their answers were really thoughtful and sweet.

Three (a.k.a. Senator Henry), however, wrote the following:

I love him, and he loves me.

You gotta love my Henry. That statement made quite an impact on me. It swiftly reminded me that it's not always about what we buy them, what we do for them, or where we take them. Sometimes, their favorite things, the things they'll remember the longest and strongest, have nothing to do with the things we, as moms, so often wrestle with—carving out time to take them to the amusement park, stomaching Peter Piper Pizza on a Friday night, or spending $75 at the movies (on a matinee no less).

Consider this quote from Bill Vaughan: "A 3-year-old child is a being who gets almost as much fun out of a fifty-six dollar set of swings as it does out of finding a small green worm."

Every so often, I have to remind myself to step back. To consciously turn off all of *my* "shoulds," whether they relate to parenting, work, or the O'mighty vegetable garden. I must lay on the floor of the family room with the kids and watch *SpongeBob* (heaven help me), *Wallace & Gromit*, and the *Barefoot Contessa* while eating popcorn and brownies.

If Henry chooses to wear the same outfit day and night for three days straight, I force myself to go with it (but I won't lie next to him after the second day).

Because I love them, and they love me.

Note: 32 seconds after I wrote this, Henry asked for a donut. I said, "We don't have donuts." He proclaimed this to be the worst day ever.

In the end, all that matters is that you love them and they love you. The rest is peripheral. I never let my kids go to bed without telling them I love them. When I catch myself thinking how cute one of them looks, I tell him (or her). When one of them sings, and I'm worried the windows might break, I tell him (or her) that I love listening to him sing. I hope never to take for granted that they know how I feel about them.

If Grace comes downstairs wearing a floral mini-skirt, a plaid top, and dangling earrings, provided it's not obscene for her to bend over, I tell her she looks adorable. She always says, "Thank you!" as though she's both surprised and thrilled to hear me say it. I can tell how much it means to her, so I do it as often as I can.

Then there's Jack, to whom I said the other day, "Jack, that shirt looks great on you!" His reply, "I know."

Alrighty then.

Rule 31
Plans Change

———— ◦∞◦ ————

"Change is inevitable, except from a vending machine."
—Robert C. Gallagher

REMEMBER THE NOT-YET-ACQUIRED-NOR-IN-HER-PARENTS'-plans-to-be-acquired dog from Rule 8? His name is Emett Charles and he's lying next to me right now.

Plans change. It's a simple rule that doesn't require much explanation. Accept it as a fact of parenting and you'll be good to go.

Rule 32
When All Else Fails, Be the Caterpillar

—◦∞◦—

"I can't change the direction of the wind, but I
can adjust my sails to always reach my destination."
—Jimmy Dean

I LOVE GREAT QUOTES; I KEEP THEM PLASTERED AROUND MY office, in my car, in the kitchen, pantry, laundry room, and anywhere else I might be when I need a boost (which is everywhere and often).

As I've mentioned, I find *New Yorker* cartoons equally necessary. Their purpose is to make me laugh, however, not think. Laughter is very necessary in my world. And easier than thought. For the record, I do not like *Far Side* cartoons. I simply don't get them. I think I'm missing a requisite brain cell or something.

At any rate, here is one of my favorite sayings:

Just when the caterpillar thought its life was over,
it became a butterfly.

It's human nature, it seems, to instinctively view what appear to be discouraging events (setbacks, inconveniences, even failures) negatively. Now, I don't believe in failure as the dictionary describes it (a person or thing that is not successful). My definition of failure: An experience in which the universe feels compelled to grab someone by her hair and whip her in an altogether different direction because she simply aren't listening!

I've learned over the years that what may be initially perceived as a setback or inconvenience often ends up proving beneficial in one way or another.

I'm reminded of the day I was running late to pick up my kids from school and hit every red light on my way there. Those red lights seemed so inconvenient, until I came upon a multi-car collision two blocks from the school and realized I likely would have been involved had I not been stopped by all of those lights.

Or the night we ran out of toilet paper at 7:30, forcing me to get out of my pajamas and into the store. But I ran into a friend in the cake aisle (it's right by the toilet paper, I swear), and she gave me a great lead for a project I was working on. I hadn't even thought to call her, yet she was the perfect person to help me.

Much more devastating, I'm reminded of those whose alarms didn't go off on September 11, 2001, causing them to miss Flight 11, Flight 93, Flight 77, or Flight 175. Or those who got stuck in traffic on July 7, 2005, and missed their train in the London subway.

What initially seemed an inconvenience on those days literally saved their lives.

So you've got this caterpillar who finds himself slowly being bound up—by what, exactly, he's not entirely sure. He then finds himself stuck inside a hot cocoon. If he finds himself this way in July in Arizona, he's probably really miserable. He may even be claustrophobic to boot.

In this scenario, he has two choices.

He can think, "This is awful. I'm hot. I can't see anything. Why is this happening to me?," feel sorry for himself, and resign himself to certain death. Or, he can think, "I don't know what is going on here. But it's cozy and dark so I'll take a nap and trust that something decent will come of it."

In the end, something much more than decent comes of it. He emerges a beautiful, free-flying butterfly. As a caterpillar, he was confined to seeing only that portion of earth that rests on (or very near to) the ground and only as widespread as his little legs enabled him to travel each day. But, as a butterfly, he can explore the world in its entirety, seeing it from whatever angle he chooses.

Most of us wake up each morning with some semblance of a plan, but we don't truly know what each day holds. We can only control so much. So, in the end, much of our sense of peace comes down to faith and attitude. To trusting that no matter what the current circumstance, there is something to be gained. To looking at each experience and wondering not why it happened, but how to turn it into something positive.

Some caterpillars are terrified by the cocooning process because they feel safer crawling on the ground, doing what feels familiar. And there are those who embrace the change, even though they are unaware of what it means—because they trust that they can only come out of it better than they went in.

The Little Engine That Could didn't know he could climb that mountain until he told himself, "I think I can." Which reminds me of another of my favorite quotes. It's a line originally coined by the Latin poet Virgil over two thousand years ago. It's the line I utter to our kids when they claim they can't or don't know how to do something. It's the line I say to *myself* when I'm ready to drive off a cliff; the seven-word mantra that grounds me when all else—including the Treat of the Moment—fails.

They can because they think they can.

It's truly what my sanity boils down to—those seven words. When people ask, How do you do it? The answer used to be, "I just do." It's changed. The answer is now, "Because I believe that I can."

When all else fails, grab a pint of Ben & Jerry's Americone Dream, be the caterpillar, and start surfing.

It's that easy.

But if nothing I've said so far works for you, consider adopting Plan B. Just do as musician and comic book writer Gerard Way suggests:

> *Be yourself, don't take anyone's shit,*
> *and never let them take you alive.*

It is with joy, thanks, and a large amount of disbelief that I send this book into bookstores, living rooms, and with any luck, Anthropologie. In no particular order, I extend my most heartfelt appreciation to the following people. No words can appropriately convey my gratitude, but I'll do my best.

Thank you to Katie Wahn, whose patience, generosity, and talent overwhelm me. It is a privilege to be your sister, and an honor to be your friend. You are welcome to call me an idiot whenever the mood strikes—just don't go more than two days without calling me.

Also, many thanks to Heather, whose last name I won't print so as to more effectively thwart the possibility—however remote—of identity theft. Thank you for the idea, the joint bank account, and the unconditional love. Now move the radicchio to the belt and let's go to Starbucks already.

Thank you to Julie Clayton, my editor, who by now likely and justifiably abhors the very sight of the comma as well as the words "flat-out" and "ironically." I appreciate you for providing tireless explanations as well as surrendering with "Do whatever you want to do" when it became clear that I was going to anyway. The only part of this manuscript you haven't reviewed a kazillion times is this Acknowledgment section; it makes me very, very nervous.

I'd also like to thank the baristas at my local Starbucks, including Craig, Sierra, Irene, Stephanie, Lillian, Michael, and Valerie. While they likely don't realize it, my family profusely thanks you as well. Without my Treat of the Moment, I would be far more difficult to live with than I already am. Lillian, when you become a dental hygienist, I'd be honored to be your first patient. Which is saying a lot. Because I'd rather birth an elephant than go to the dentist.

Thank you to every inspiring, motivating, and goosebump-producing song and YouTube video, specifically anything by Beyonce or an incredible drummer under the age of four. When necessary, you stirred up whatever needed to be stirred up in me in order to avert a month-long case of writer's block.

Thank you to Anthropologie for never ceasing to make me happy, even though I can't afford any of your wares beyond a final clearance teacup. But I do love my teacups.

To Jerry from Body Creations in Glendale, Arizona, thank you for completing the (surprisingly painless) piercing of my nose the day this manuscript was declared ready to go to print. You provided the perfect final punctuation mark. I think I've now pierced everything I'm going to pierce, but I'll surely recommend you to anyone else looking to take the plunge.

To all the women who've written me in the midst of a trying hour, I'm flattered and humbled by your faith in me—and a bit terrified by it at the same time. May you acknowledge and celebrate your uniqueness each and every day.

To Grace, Jack, Henry, George, and Nina, I thank you and appreciate you for accepting that I can only sit with a Monopoly or Sorry board for so long and loving me anyway. I will love each of you for eternity plus one day. No matter how many books I write, how big an organic carrot I produce, or how many times I may have the opportunity to ride on the back of Bret Michaels' motorcyle, the five of you will forever remain my greatest joys—even when you drop your pants in public, call each other expletives I'm certain you didn't learn from me, and insist that one of the dogs drew the Tic-Tac-Toe board on the couch.

And David, thank you for being you. For giving me all the space in the world to be me. For photographing the beauty that is our life with a talent that is nothing short of God-given. For learning not to be surprised by anything. At all. Ever. You are, quite simply, My Wonderwall.

ABOUT THE AUTHOR

Elizabeth Lyons is many things: mom, wife, friend, lunch maker, chauffeur, hostage negotiator, author, on-call plumber, tile layer, guitar student, window washer, product designer, and on and on.

One thing she is *not* is Superwoman.

She simply demands the right to do things her way—a way that often defies even the most creative imaginations—and she strives to inspire others to do things *their* way (once they figure out what their way is!).

Elizabeth lives in Arizona with her husband, five kids, two dogs, a fish called Wanda, four barely surviving organic gardens, and whatever (or whomever) else has taken up residence with them since this manuscript went to print.

She claims this is the last book she'll write (which she also claimed the last time).

www.ElizabethLyons.com